M000266771

VALIDATION FOR
THE CHILD-HEART PROCESS

"Using compelling case examples and aspects of her own vulnerable healing journey, Dr. Uemura's insightful book helps people remain open to the unexpected and teaches them how to more effectively steward their own healing journeys. This book and the accessible, user-friendly methodology contained within it offers a valuable addition to the self-help and self-inquiry literature."

—Harvey L. Schwartz, PhD, Author of
The Alchemy of Wolves and Sheep
and *Dialogues with Forgotten Voices*

"Thank you . . . It's not the first time my adult accessed my inner child that way. But it sure got me there faster than the twenty-odd years of extensive research, fifty years of soul searching, and the list of therapies I've done. The other great piece is that I know what still gets in my way."

—Holistic massage therapist

"My sessions with Anne have been priceless . . . It has been beautiful work . . . healed a part of my inner child that needed to be brought home and nurtured . . . done with ease and great love . . . My life feels richer and more complete . . . have a greater depth of peace."

—Debbie Healy, Reiki Master

"Really awesome, powerful, effective process you have, Anne. I shifted out of emotional turmoil by connecting compassionately with a young part, soothing and giving myself what I didn't receive as a child."

—Brianna Ho Delott, Spiritual Counselor

"Anne, just want to thank you for the powerful and healing sessions this morning. I feel so light and grounded and joyful. I guess I need days to digest and absorb all that . . . this will be a healing weekend. Thank you!"

—Longtime client

"Through the Child Heart work I've done with Anne, I've been able to access preverbal memory. The power of connecting with such deep memory and having it witnessed with the loving, compassionate presence of another has actively reconfigured my internal psychological and emotional construct. I literally feel as though I am another person . . . I feel a new freedom and buoyancy. A sense of possibility and movement.

"This is magical work. I sense it is, at least for now, ongoing. Meanwhile, I am hugely grateful to Anne and the Child-Heart method."

—Diane, whose sessions appear in several chapters.

"The sessions have been a wonderful addition to my other tools. They provide a quick, easy method to allow the 'child' parts that wish to be heard to come forward and provide the information that needs to be integrated. Even though I've been dedicated to the work for a long time, I'm not always able to access what needs to come forward 'right now.' It is so simple to look into the heart and see who is there. I love it! I have found that those parts that have presented have been very relevant to the other processes going on in my life . . . I am drawn to simplicity so this appeals to me very much. Some of the parts coming forward have been a complete surprise . . . I can see myself utilizing this process for the rest of my days."

—Siobhan MacMahon, Shamanic Healer

"Anne's inner child work allows you to safely engage with your own hurt child, revealing obstacles to your heart's desire and helping you clear those obstacles to live more fully and freely. Inner work is especially important for those of us who are healers: the clearer we are, the more the Light can channel through us to reach others. Anne is a compassionate, wise, and truly gifted healer who has synthesized her years of practice as a psychologist and energy healer to now offer the world this brilliant yet simple technique for moving beyond our defenses and releasing that which binds us."

—Kali-Ki Reiki® Founder, Teacher,
and Master Joni Dittrich, PhD

LISTEN TO THE CRIES OF YOUR HEART

THE CHILD-HEART PATH TO YOUR INNER CHILD

Anne K. Uemura, PhD

To Priestess sister Linda,
I hope the reading of
these pages will add to
your wise large heart.
Blessings
Much love,
Anne

始 HAJIME
PUBLICATIONS

Copyright©2016 Anne K. Uemura, PhD.

All rights reserved. No part of this publication may be reproduced, distributed or transmitted in any form or by any means, including photocopying, recording, or other electronic or mechanical methods, without the prior written permission of the publisher, except in the case of brief quotations embodied in critical reviews and certain other noncommercial uses permitted by copyright law. For permission requests, write to the publisher, addressed "Attention: Permissions Coordinator," at the address below.

The author and publisher make no representation or warranties with respect to the accuracy, applicability, fitness, or completeness of the contents of this Program. The information contained in this Program is strictly for educational purposes. Some names and identifying details have been changed to protect the privacy of individuals.

This book is not intended as a substitute for the medical advice of physicians. The reader should regularly consult a physician in matters relating to his/her health and particularly with respect to any symptoms that may require diagnosis or medical attention.

Ordering Information:

Quantity sales. Special discounts are available on quantity purchases by corporations, associations, and others. For details, contact the "Special Sales Dept" at Hajime Resources Publishing, 1438 Oak St., Napa, CA 94559-3311

Cover illustration ©2016 Karen Nagano, www.karennagano.com
Editing by Candace Johnson, Change It Up Editing
Author photograph by Jordan Williams Photography
Book cover design by Miguel Kilantang,
    http://migzworks.wix.com/migzworks
Book Layout and typesetting by grzegorzlaszczyk.pl

"A Short Story" ©2016 Paulette Litz, used with permission
"Song of Thanks" ©2016 Doug Brozell, used with permission
"The Undefended Heart" ©2016 Marianne Lyon, used with permission

Listen to the Cries of Your Heart/ Anne K. Uemura, PhD —1st ed.

ISBN 978-0-9976545-2-3

CONTENTS

Foreword   1

Acknowledgments   3

Introduction   5

[1] Why You Should Listen to the Cries of Your Heart   17

[2] Gaining Access to the Two-Year-Old
    through Her Tantrums   35

[3] Details of the Child-Heart Method   51

[4] Samples of Full Child-Heart Sessions   73

[5] Beliefs as Access Points to the Child-Selves   87

[6] Strategies Born from Wounds   105

[7] How the Young Self Defends   121

[8] Final Thoughts on the Child-Heart Method   135

Thank You!   147

Additional Resources   149

Appendix   151

References   161

Index   163

About the Author   173

FOREWORD

For those of you who have ever had times when you felt totally alone and didn't know where to turn, when you felt betrayed by a friend and cut to the core, when you felt that you could never find joy again, or when you felt overwhelmed with the responsibilities of life, Anne's insights in this book reassure you that your journey is not in vain and that the rewards can be far greater than you could ever have anticipated.

Each of us is born with the natural tendency to focus on the joy and happiness around and within us, but somehow we lose that ability along the way. As children, our imaginations flourished, and we knew how to use them. Because of the beliefs that were programmed into us, we perceived the world then much differently than we perceive it today.

So what happened? Did we reach a certain age when the enchantment of life just vanished? Not at all; that enchantment is still there and buried within. We were simply taught an incorrect philosophy that contradicts who we are at the core. We were taught to believe in things like competition, sickness, limitation, guilt, fear, and scarcity. As we were taught these things, they became a part of our lives. We were taught that success, money, material things, competing to get ahead, and being right were more important than self-love and following our heart's desire.

In this book, Anne demonstrates the power of listening to the cries of your heart. She shows us that the child-like spirit and self-love are always within us. They cannot be destroyed. They are simply hidden, ready to be awakened.

A few years ago a reader of my book *Rings of Truth* emailed me, asking if certain parts of my story were true. Over a few days of email communication and after I shared with him the truth behind each story, he asked, "Why you, Jim? Why were you chosen to share this work and not me or someone else?"

My response was, "Why not me?"

I told him that I believe we are all teachers and students. We are all here to learn from one another.

Although I believe it is up to each of us as individuals to work toward self-healing by addressing our own emotional dramas, exercising our willpower, and accessing the power of choice that has been gifted us, at times we may also find a need to seek out others for help, to help direct us toward the life our heart cries out for us to live.

Often though, there are healers who go absolutely unnoticed until the timing is right for their introduction to the world . . . until time, fate, and circumstances bring them to light. Anne Uemura is that kind of healer.

Certainly Anne's experiences shaped the outcome of her life. But more important, how she chose to handle those experiences is what made her the woman she is today: an emotional healer and an example of what can be done under unfortunate circumstances.

Through Anne's personal experiences, she shows you how to meet each personal challenge head-on, identify your upsetting emotions, and remove the layers of false beliefs. Everyone should read this book. It will be a powerful, emotional, life-changing experience. In this book, Anne shines a light on the path ahead for each of us to follow.

—Jim Britt, inspirational keynote speaker,
success coach, and author of thirteen bestselling books
including *Rings of Truth* and *The Change*

ACKNOWLEDGMENTS

I have many to acknowledge for their participation in the project I'm calling the Child-Heart Method. *Listen to the Cries of Your Heart* would not exist were it not for the belief that Jim Britt and Jim Lutes expressed in me when they invited me to be a coauthor in *Change Book #8.*

I appreciate my wonderful family of three sisters (Ellen, Ella, and Edie), my two children (Blandon and Laurice), my daughter-in-law (Cristina), and my grandchildren (Noelani and Alana). I love each dearly, and know they provide a foundation I am blessed to have in my life.

A heartfelt thank you to my support "team" for the creation of *Listen to the Cries of Your Heart,* including Doug Brozell, MD, who read and edited countless versions of my manuscript and provided support in many ways; Harvey L. Schwartz, PhD, Mavis Tsai, PhD, and Joni Dittrich, PhD, my colleagues and longtime friends; and other soul friends who read chapters, encouraged me, and/or participated in sessions, especially Kristi Johnson, Brianna Ho Delott, Siobhan MacMahon, and Karen Nagano.

I cannot thank my superb editor, Candace Johnson, enough for her warm and constant support, skillful re-organization, and questions and comments that masterfully reshaped the content of this book.

I am also deeply and especially grateful also to Child-Heart workshop participants and clients who trusted me to orient and guide them to connect with their child-selves. The material in *Listen to the Cries of Your Heart* is richer and more complete because of what I learned from them and what they were willing to share with readers of this book.

I am not alone in recognizing that I stand on the shoulders of many whose wisdom and knowledge informed and inspired me. I appreciate all of my many teachers, beginning with Dr. Brian Weiss, Barbara Brennan and her faculty, Barbara Johnson of the Open Door community, others I mention in the book, and especially Miranda Macpherson, my current spiritual teacher extraordinaire.

INTRODUCTION

Do you remember how you felt in some young playground experience when the children were choosing teams and everyone else's name was called but yours? Or how you reacted when hearing about a party to which you weren't invited? Or how, when you went to a family gathering, a first date, or an interview, you very soon felt as though the wrong you had shown up?

Such events triggered and upset you because they touched your wounded heart.

Picture the unrestrained expression of unmet needs from a baby or toddler. The intensity and distress conveyed in such outbursts pierce through you. Though your first instinctive response may be to turn away, there's no denying that the tantrum seizes your attention.

When you were young and threw tantrums, you were probably not encouraged to continue, especially in public. Those around you let you know that it wasn't okay, and you quickly learned to quiet your distress.

As an adult, you may believe that you are too grown up to throw tantrums. Would it surprise you to realize that every time you get upset, you are throwing a "quiet" tantrum? Like the two-year-old, you aren't getting what you want. Your needs aren't being met. Being upset is an expression of a wounded heart crying out in the adult.

No matter where or when we began our lives, no matter how wonderful our parents are, no one escapes wounding in the first years of life. There is always an interruption—subtle or dramatic, momentary or prolonged—in our infant and toddler needs being met.

These moments, minutes, or days of separation from comfort and love impact us deeply, whether they came from the birth of a sibling, adoption, divorce, illness or death in the family, the absence of mother for whatever reason, or the loss of anyone significant to you.

The effects of these disruptions of safety and care on a young heart vary. *Listen to the Cries of Your Heart* is for those who grew up in normal or dysfunctional families and seem to function well as adults. (When the wounds come from violence and torture, children often develop psychological disorders which are beyond the scope of this book).

In Child-Heart sessions with individuals from nurturing families, several child-selves are often present in one individual. When traumatized, a child-self splits off, holding particular memories and secret traumas in the heart. To achieve a full integration, to become whole, these split-off parts need full attention.

A young-self who was hurt as a vulnerable young child hides overwhelming, difficult feelings because the pain and negative feelings seem unbearable. In addition, "decisions" about beliefs, defenses, and strategies result as a way to make sense out of life. A now-defended heart guides the young child through childhood, adolescence, and adulthood.

You may not remember the early wounds because you see that your childhood was good or even "perfect." Yet no matter how you view your past, if you look with openness you will find evidence of wounding.

These deep hurts of the defended heart from early childhood, adolescence, and adulthood are addressed by the Child-Heart method. Its aim is to gather the child-hearts for integration. Its aim is to gather the wounded and defended child-hearts—no matter when the trauma occurred—to create wholeness and freedom.

The Child-Heart method includes:

- **creating** what I call the *imaginal* world through deep relaxation. You call forth a memory of a safe place, a haven for comfort, which increases a sense of safety. Or as the adult you can create a place of safety. Safety is increased by the invocation of what is "most sacred" at the moment.
- **inviting** a child-self, called by her connection to a chronic emotion, situation, belief, or strategy, to appear. Or you may extend an open invitation to any child-self ready to come forth with secrets to share.
- **being present** to her until you make a connection and then witnessing and meeting with compassion what is in her heart. Your presence changes her sense of aloneness; your messages to her are "antidotes" for her beliefs that change her. You will see signs in her that an authentic connection occurred.
- **committing** to a relationship with all young-selves to acknowledge the signs of them in everyday life, as well as to spend time meeting their hearts.

Who Am I?

I am a clinical psychologist in practice for more than thirty years, including working and retiring as a counseling psychologist at University of California-Berkeley. Later I expanded my offerings when I became a certified life coach. Curiosity led me to become a healer in several traditions, among them Reiki as a Reiki Master, and a certified healing science practitioner of the Barbara Brennan School of Healing.

Ever a student of both cutting-edge technologies and ancient teaching, I've trained with many teachers because no one practice or approach satisfied me. Nothing provided the wholeness or healing of the soul and heart that I was seeking.

The creation of the Child-Heart method is the result of everything I've learned, practiced, and experienced over five decades. The method is unique because it combines aspects of many of my studies.

It has, for example, the influence of the Socratic method of inquiry from my philosophy studies. Elements of my study with the Toltecs (of Don Miguel's lineage), Barbara Johnson of the Open Door community, the Hawaiian system of Ho'oponopono, Dr. Brian Weiss's past regressions, Chris Howard's neurological repatterning, *A Course in Miracles*, Dr. Joni Dittrich's DROPPP (deep release of persistent pain patterns), and my spiritual teacher, Miranda Macpherson, have informed the ingredients of the Child-Heart method.

While others in the self-empowerment niche address your beliefs and your mind, I offer this work focused on the heart. There is no question that your beliefs are the reason you see the world, life, and yourself as you do. However, when you use only your mind to change your beliefs, you fail to make significant changes because the beliefs are in the subconscious and have their source in the heart.

Remember that advertising rests on the power of emotions. The heart is stronger than the mind in its effect on decisions. This is why the Child-Heart purpose is to meet the young heart fully with your adult heart.

It was exciting to feel my cumulative wisdom and intuitive gifts guide me in assembling the content of the original chapter in *Change Book 8*. Now delight and inspiration fill me as I write an entire book on the subject of how our inner children are calling to us. But more, it seemed natural to me to devise a way of *therapeutically meeting* the two-year-old. This is how the Child-Heart method was born.

What Is the Child-Heart Method?

The Child-Heart method begins by finding the signs of the *two-year-old*, the name I've chosen for our young-selves. I will use "two-year-old" to describe the young parts through early years as a toddler, a baby, even an embryo, and refer to "her" for ease of reading.

For some, it's easy to notice the times when being upset indicate a temper tantrum as an adult: "I am not getting what I need!" "I am not getting my way!" For others, the two-year-old is quiet and is found in beliefs about being "not good enough," needing to be "perfect," or "pleasing everyone." Or it can manifest in strategies of feeling secure with the perfect career or spouse, or doing whatever is needed to control/manipulate someone.

Many ignore or are deaf to the cries of the inner child because of fear. This is understandable since fear can be uncomfortable to feel as well as debilitating and sometimes overwhelming. Moreover, when you lack information about the influence of the inner child on your life and don't have a solution, *a way to change your situation*, it's easy to deny its importance. I've also learned that many child-selves hide their fear, which may subconsciously cause the adult at some level to feel afraid to change.

Some numb themselves with busyness or addictions such as eating, shopping, exercise, smoking, drugs, or drinking. It's not surprising that long neglected emotional pain bursts out as a physical symptom that you can't ignore. Before that happens to you, please move away from your numbing routines and what distracts you.

Once you have access points through a chronic emotion, or situations that result in overreaction, you can begin to contact and build a relationship to an inner child. The intention is to meet a young-self with your presence, curiosity, compassion, and love.

There is no agenda except *to be present* as a kind witness to what the young child holds in her heart: the hurt, fears, anguish, sadness, bewilderment, anger, helplessness, and feelings of being unsafe and alone—the reactions to an early wound.

You can use the same process to find inner selves who originally "decided" on views of who they are, what their lives and their world would look like, and how they would survive. These are the beliefs, the defenses or strategies, the layers of protection that ensure they will never hurt again.

Once you acknowledge and fully meet your young-self, she won't need to cry out to you as often, if at all. A connection with you has given her a radically different experience—a corrective or reparative experience. The adult's presence can end her isolation. The child-self has shown you her secrets and revealed what she hid. It's as if the sharing of her heart's secrets dissolves her sense of separation. She has no reason to remain disconnected. As a result, Child-Heart sessions can end with a sense of the young one merging into the adult.

Listen to the Cries of Your Heart is not for the fainthearted. It asks you to take time to examine your life and learn your heart's messages by helping you identify your upsetting emotions, beliefs, strategies, and defenses. We use these signs from the young hearts as access points—the doors back to each young-self.

In most chapters, you will find exercises and self-inquiry questions to prepare you to use the Child-Heart method on your own. Your self-reflection will reveal how the upsetting emotions and elements of the layers of protection (beliefs, strategies, and beliefs) are all interrelated and explain how you live and why you have the life you have.

For example, when you realize that you feel bad because someone pointed out a mistake you made, you can see the connection between your emotion (feeling bad or ashamed) and your belief ("You aren't good enough"). You may notice that you avoid saying what you think because others may not like you for being truthful. You've discovered a strategy (be a people pleaser to have them like you) connected to a belief ("I'm good/worthy only if someone approves of me").

Remember, beliefs that limit how you regard yourself and your possibilities in the world come from a very young place. Limiting strategies that define your patterns of behavior (examples include taking control of most situations; trying to please everyone; not trusting anyone) also come from immature reasoning. They are rigid and habitual.

All of these—intense feelings, limiting beliefs, and strategies—indicate the presence of a wounded heart and therefore provide a way to access the young-self in the Child-Heart process. For some, the cries can be physical symptoms, such as chronic fatigue syndrome or irritable bowel syndrome (IBS), or emotional distress such as anxiety and depression.

Within these chapters, I will guide you to an expansive understanding of how you came to be who you are with your current life situation. The information and method provide the kind of guidance you have yearned for—one that leads you to a deeper place within you. The Child-Heart method guides you to the child-selves who hold a broken piece of your heart. By compassionately connecting with each, you gather the child-selves home for wholeness.

~

The first basic ingredient of this book is my story: what happened when I didn't listen to the cries of my own heart, and what happens when I do. My story began when I was about seven years old, and it continues as I write on this topic now. The cries of my heart were my deep needs or longings that appeared unexpectedly throughout my life. For others, the cries can be physical symptoms, such as cancer or a heart attack or emotional distress such as panic attacks and chronic anger.

Another ingredient is the stories of the workshop participants, friends, and clients who have used the Child-Heart method that I describe. I extend my immense gratitude to these courageous, generous and willing individuals who trusted me to guide them through this process of accessing a source of their current life challenges.

The third ingredient is background information: the results of study, training, and practices from my whole adult life. As I described earlier, the influences began with the Socratic method of self-inquiry, learned in my philosophy undergraduate major and that I taught in college classes. They continue today with enlightening insights from my spiritual practice with Miranda Macpherson that focuses on returning to the undefended heart.

You are attracted to *Listen to the Cries of Your Heart* for a reason. You may not know exactly what has drawn you to these pages. Be curious because all profit by moving toward undefended hearts by welcoming and facing what is uncomfortable right now in order to become more alive, to awaken.

Listen to the Cries of Your Heart is written for those who:

- recognize that they suffer from childhood wounding and haven't found a way to move beyond the consequences of such hurts of their inner child. Some of these individuals know well that their family environment was hurtful and/or abusive. For others, the wounding was subtler, with sources in family challenges of the birth of siblings, adoption, fighting, illness, and death in their early home environment.
- have failed to find in the self-help and self-empowerment literature what truly will bring them the happiness and success in living they seek. They are still bewildered and plagued by limiting beliefs that cause suffering, such as low self-esteem and feeling undeserving, or are trapped with strategies of giving and pleasing that leave them unfulfilled.

- are devoted to their spiritual path but are honest enough to recognize that only their minds have changed and everything at the core remains the same. A friend recently shared, "I've had a spiritual practice for over twenty-one years and only recently realized that my spiritual and metaphysical practices aren't enough. I have to face the trauma and abuse of my early years."

The Child-Heart Method emphasizes relationship. It's not a one-time meeting with the expectation that you need to know only one child-self and provide one corrective experience. Rather, it is a relationship that continues until you see, welcome, witness, and integrate sufficient number of child-selves.

When you come to know and acknowledge one child-self, you may notice a difference in your life. The quality of your life begins to radically change only when you gather most of your "lost children."

I certainly realize that inner child work has been in the self-help and psychology literature for decades. Many experts have written articles and books, including Carl Jung with the Divine Child archetype, Hugh Missildine, MD, with his "inner child of the past," art therapist Dr. Lucia Capacchione, who has written extensively on reparenting the inner child, and John Bradshaw's "wounded inner child." The healing or therapeutic techniques offered reflect the experiences and training of each expert, just as the Child-Heart method does.

I trust that this book will be helpful to you because every expert on the inner child agrees that **all** need to attend to the cries of their hearts—the voices of the wounded child. With healers and therapists, no one practitioner is a good match for all clients. Similarly, one inner child method can be helpful to one and not be right for another. It's a question of your readiness and whether my words and spirit touch you.

What may be unique is that the actual method itself begins with the direct creation of the work's context in the place or space of imagination. A strong base in safety is important, and the inclusion of the sacred adds power to the imaginal place.

It's also not a matter of providing immediate comfort with words or a hug to the inner child. Rather, there is emphasis on the adult witnessing and accepting with presence and compassion *the intolerable pain and secrets in the child's heart.*

It's not only about meeting the wounded heart, but also about going deeper—building enough connection so the secrets are shared for the first time. Heart to heart. Without this step, there is no reparative experience and the child-heart remains unchanged.

Listen to the Cries of Your Heart also insists on *a committed relationship* with the inner child. Without one, the child-parts have an additional abandonment experience with heart-secrets untouched.

I offer this material as a gift from the accumulation of decades of my experience, training, study, and practice as described above. I am adding my voice at this time to all who hear the call to return home to the heart, a place of peace and love.

I see myself as the formulator of the Child-Heart method as well as the first experimenter, and the experiences of others have validated this process. The experiences that follow are those from my Child-Heart workshops, my private practice, and dear friends. The workshops run from three to five hours, including information about the method as well as exercises to familiarize attendees with the process of meeting a child-self.

It takes courage to begin the process of removing the layers of protection created by the young child to protect you from further hurt. The protection has worked, more or less effectively, to shield and prevent you from further harm. But it has also created a wall around your heart that limits your expression of your full potential. Patience, persistence, courage, and trust are required to move beyond these walls of defense.

What is also essential is that you:

- believe that you are more much than who you know yourself to be right now,
- recognize that you deeply long for abiding peace and true love, and
- want the fullness of what life offers, to give freedom to your inner child with her spontaneity, creativity, and aliveness.

Please join me on a path to your original undefended heart. You won't be upset as often. Fears diminish. Beliefs and strategies become less automatic. You make new decisions or choices. You see things differently. These changes allow for freedom and creativity, relief and joy because you found in your undefended heart a source of lasting peace, unconditional love, and undeniable joy.

You will encounter many questions in the following chapters, and some chapters end with "Exercises" to prepare you for the Child-Heart method. These questions are for your self-reflection—a journal would be a perfect purchase for yourself. I encourage you to create time, even if it's only fifteen minutes a day—perhaps before going to bed or upon rising in the morning—to spend with yourself. Additional journaling questions are available in Additional Resources.

If you don't commit this time for yourself, it's easy to continue being on the gerbil wheel of your ingrained patterns. Remember the words of the very wise Albert Einstein: Doing the same things over and over again and expecting different results is the definition of insanity.

Listen to the Cries of Your Heart directs you to your heart, the center of your emotional life and intelligence as well the seat of the soul. Your heart contains important answers you seek. The potential to clear the confusion, powerlessness, and suffering that are debilitating burdens lies within you—in the undefended heart. Without the layers of protection around your heart, you will know your original innocence, joy, peace, and wisdom. It is time for heart-centered living.

It is time to listen to the cries of your heart.

WHY YOU SHOULD LISTEN TO THE CRIES OF YOUR HEART

The cries of your heart come in different forms as you've learned in the Introduction. They are most apparent when you are upset because your *needs and expectations* aren't met. You feel more than a little disappointed, angry, or anxious. These feelings linger or may be overreactions to a situation that wouldn't disturb others. These upsetting feelings are cries indicating that an early wound has been touched.

For some, the *deep needs or longings of the heart* cry out for notice. They may consciously or unconsciously drive you to seek success or fame, take physical or emotional risks, seek spiritual enlightenment, or find security wherever you can.

Some of you can immediately identify the cries of the heart and understand what these cries are. For others, recognizing your heart's cries may be a bit more challenging. You will learn how your heart's cries manifest as you read through these chapters.

More essential perhaps is to learn the *importance* of listening to the cries of your heart: they are cries from a wounded self that needs attention. When these cries are ignored, your life remains fundamentally unchanged and your full potential untapped. More sadly, the "lost inner children" remain isolated and forgotten.

What Are the "Cries of Your Heart"?

For one courageous soul, the cries showed up dramatically in the cancer that eventually took her life. Lynn was referred to me by a fellow spiritual counselor who was exhausted by Lynn's needs for support when her cancer treatments weren't working. We had six sessions within eight days before her travels interrupted our contact.

In Lynn's Child-Heart sessions we learned together how her young heart felt swallowed up and invaded by the "darkness" coming from three members of her family. In her vulnerable and difficult childhood years, her young-self could not hold on to her father's love.

There had been a clear cry fifteen years earlier in her life when she, a very competent and courageous professional, fell apart after her father died. She developed brain fog as well as other symptoms common with Chronic Fatigue Syndrome that was her diagnosis.

She had an incredible need to know and feel love that was absent for her most of her life. Although she was able to connect with several child-selves, in six sessions there wasn't enough time for her to be with the child-heart that knew the pain of having lost her father's love.

Sadly, a week after our last session I heard from her brother that Lynn had passed.

I know Diane as a member of a group we belonged to for years. She said yes to a Child-Heart workshop after learning about its title and without reading its description. I've only become more acquainted with her because of her experiences with the Child-Heart method. For Diane (whose full story comes later), the cries were apparent most every day of her adult life.

She awakened to anxiety and terror most mornings. It took her twenty minutes to pull herself together and live an admirably productive and full life. Diane used two workshop and five individual Child-Heart sessions to find seven of the important child-selves she had suppressed.

Lee's story is a bit different. I know Lee through a women's group I ran for a few years. She occasionally had individual sessions for particular issues. None of these "complaints" revealed the presence of a wounded heart. Those who know her as a colleague and friend love and admire her. Her warm personality and high competence are valued in her career as well. Only in a Child-Heart workshop did she identify a "vague feeling" that came up, which was a cry from her heart.

As you can gather, the cries of the heart can appear as physical symptoms, such as a difficult diagnosis as cancer or Chronic Fatigue Syndrome. They can appear as emotional signs--feelings of upset such as anxiety, anger, fear, jealousy, or helplessness. For many, the cries are buried by adult activities—responsibilities and busyness.

In all their doing, adults often feel the sense of feeling overwhelmed and stressed by the demands of their lives. Stress could be how the child is saying, "Enough, please attend to me and my (your) heart."

I remember the first cry of my heart. My Japanese-American family of four girls was blessed to live in an idyllic, luscious valley in Nuuanu on the Island of Oahu. All of us sisters treasure the memory of playing in the stream that flowed at the bottom of the mountain near our home, and in the surrounding fields and forests. We played in the *hau* trees, a natural jungle gym, knocked ripe guavas from the trees overhanging the stream and gathered them for our grandmother to make jam, waited impatiently each year for the common mango to ripen in the groves around the property, and feasted on *ohea*, a wild mountain apple, the flavor of which is indescribable.

Yet in that paradise, I met a "serpent." I was eight years old and disturbed by what a ten-year-old neighbor boy had done to me in my private parts. Afterward, feeling dirty, guilty, and confused, I looked up into the Hawaiian sky and asked, "God, where are you?" I needed to know I wasn't bad, that I was okay, and that I wasn't alone.

This is an instance of how the young heart cries out of confusion, fear, and feeling tainted with darkness, believing she is alone and unsupported. In the Child-Heart sessions you read about later, difficult feelings like these and more hide as secrets in the heart.

No answer came for me then, but that need for God surfaced when as a teenager I responded to the seductive message of evangelical Christians and accepted Christ as my Savior. For years I appreciated the camaraderie of my Christian friends, but after a while the fellowship wasn't enough. Although my mind said the theology embraced by the fellowship was limited, it was my soul that wasn't satisfied. I moved on.

I forgot my cry for God for most of my adult life. My days filled with school, college, a growing family, studying for a doctoral degree, working again full time, and being a single mom. Four decades later, in my third year of attending Barbara Brennan Healing School (BBSH), I remembered this cry of the child-me. The dean of our class announced that the year would be devoted to our relationship to the Divine. Tears rolled down my cheeks as I remembered my early need to come home to God.

How could I have forgotten?

The Why

If you disregard or don't recognize the cries of your heart, you risk missing the fullness of what life offers. You remain a prisoner within the walls of protection you've built around your heart. While your heart is defended with strategies to deal with life that may or may not be effective, you don't have access to the depth of what your heart offers. You will never know your soul purpose or what your true potential is.

My story is an illustration of living a life with a highly defended heart, and with well-hidden beliefs of "not deserving," harboring secret (even from myself) feelings of being lost and alone, with strategies of compliance to stay safe and not be a target, and with perfectionism that goaded me and left me always unsatisfied with anything I did. I use examples from my life to illustrate how beliefs, defenses, and strategies come from the young and wounded heart. Later chapters contain full information for you on how to discover the other signs of protection created by your young-self.

With a PhD in clinical psychology and certifications in many training programs as a healer and life coach, and having a stable emotional life, I can pass as a picture of "success." But for many years, I was like an automaton with fully programmed responses.

After hundreds of hours of therapy, coaching, healing (all required by the programs I was in), and spiritual practice, I still hadn't touched my wounded heart to release my full truth and authority. However, once I connected with my child-selves, the layers of protection melted away, and today I am finally experiencing freedom, truth, wisdom, peace, and even joy.

That's the short story—a summary. What follows is the longer answer to why *you* must listen to the cries of your heart. When the cries of your heart fully express the pain, desperation, and longings that your heart contains, you can't help but pay attention.

Because we've had to mute our heart's cries, my message to you is this: *listen for* the cries of your heart. One way of listening is to pay attention to when you are upset, in crisis, overwhelmed, or feeling in need of rescue. Unless you make the time to listen (guidance for listening will be provided through journaling questions), you will miss important messages that give your life direction, help free you from your current struggles and challenges, and lead you to your true longings. When you hear and attend to the cries of your heart, you can come to know who you really are. Through the Child-Heart method, I will guide you to find what you long for— abiding peace and love, wisdom to guide you, uplifting joy, your creative potential, and freedom.

"I'm finally home" is what recent Child-Heart respondents have said after integrating important child-selves. After sufficient numbers of child-heart sessions, some conducted on their own, and others guided by me, these respondents describe with awe how different they feel.

For example, one described feeling free from the rigid patterns of perfectionism that caused her to over prepare her whole adult life. Another stated that she's now free from the resentment and anger she held for years against her mother. "I no longer feel this free-floating anxiety that I've experienced for years," reported a third.

Are You Distracted?

I don't believe I am the only one who heard what my heart needed and then became distracted by life. Do you have a similar story? Are your days filled with endless stimuli that bombard your ears so you cannot tune into your heart's deep messages?

When you consider, as you might right now, what you listen to, what do all the familiar sounds of your world, your family, workplace, community, and perhaps the talk from TV and radio *mean to you*?

How about what happens in your mind? Are you in your head, thinking most of the time, reading or mulling over an incident or someone's story? How much time do you spend deeply or genuinely listening to something or someone—most importantly, yourself—with *your full attention*?

If you could listen deeply to yourself, would you hear what really matters to you? What are your dreams? What do you truly need? What are the cries of your heart?

Consider all these questions: do you scan them quickly or do you pause to reflect? They are here for you to think about, but I understand that right now you may not have time to reflect. That is why journaling will be an important part of what you can do with this material. Highlight or otherwise mark questions that appear in these pages for reflection in your time for self-inquiry.

Commitment to Self-Inquiry

One of the first steps in using this book for self-improvement is making time to be with yourself and to give yourself full attention. You can start with any of the questions I pose in this and other chapters to examine your life.

As I mention in the Introduction, at the end of most chapters are questions and exercises to help prepare you for the Child-Heart method. Most important of all, commit to spend at least fifteen minutes a day with yourself. Choose a time when you can ensure there is no interruption. This early commitment will help you prepare to communicate with your inner children. You're practicing the first step in self-care.

Buying a journal is another commitment that brings you closer to spending time with yourself. Setting up times in the week, *appointments with yourself* that you honor as you would any other appointment, is yet another step toward self-empowerment. One Child-Heart workshop participant put it this way: "My inner child surely deserves my time equal to or more than what I commit to my student clients."

Life Transitions and the Cries

At different times in each of our lives, we can hear the cries of our hearts—especially when events in our lives shock us. We become fearful, feel our helplessness, voice our pain, and feel unable to cope, such as in dramatic life-threatening events like accidents, and health issues like cancer and heart attacks.

The many transitions of life expose our vulnerabilities. From being a child to becoming an adult; getting married or divorced; becoming a single parent; moving from employment to unemployment; slipping from wellness into illness; or losing a loved one, these dramatic events throw us off our usual rhythm so that we *can* hear our heart's cries. Transition events too, like weddings and funerals, are notorious for eliciting family wounds.

Well-meaning friends and family may tell us to cope with these passages. "Grief will pass." "What you want will show up." We are encouraged to take a passive role, keep our chin up, and see what life brings. Instead, I suggest you see these times of disruptions and confusion as opportunities to mine for treasure.

In his book *Cancer as a Turning Point,* psychotherapist Lawrence LeShan wrote about clients who ignored the cries of their heart until cancer woke them up. Dr. LeShan worked with his patients to discover what wasn't working in their lives, and to build on what gave them a sense of being alive—activities that were meaningful and inspiring to each.

In my training to become a healer, I learned that conflicts unattended at the mental, emotional, and spiritual levels appear on the physical level. When an alarm, such as a frightening diagnosis or a heart attack sounds, many wake up to pay attention—but usually attend to the *physical* resolution of the illness. Most ignore important issues of the heart or soul.

I still remember two stories I read in Dr. LeShan's book decades ago. The first is about a woman in her seventies who learned in her therapy sessions that she had forgotten about her love of opera most of her life. Instead she devoted her life to her children, even after they were adults. Once she decided to create an independent life for herself based on her love of opera, her cancer went into remission.

The second story is about a young and talented married woman who learned in therapy that she had deferred her life to her husband. She suspected that her artistic career threatened her husband. Therefore, she held back on her gift, a sacrifice she was willing to make. Though it seemed clear that this decision to invest in her husband's life instead of her own was the source of the cancer, she chose not to focus on herself, and she died from cancer.

LeShan's work illustrates how necessary it is to attend to more than the physical aspects of a diagnosis. The theme of his clients' lives was living someone else's life, not their own—a life that didn't express their uniqueness and individuality. From the Child-Heart perspective they ignored the needs of their heart.

When the Cries of the Heart Go Unheard

As you explore the questions and examine your life through self-inquiry as I suggest, you will begin to see how you made choices or complied with demands because of unconscious needs of your heart. For example, you may see that you chose a career path that your family expected and turned away from something more aligned to who you are—because you were unconsciously plagued by a feeling of being "not good enough" or by the strategy of pleasing. Or that you chose to marry far too young because you desperately needed love.

In short, even if you ignore the cries of your heart, you probably still respond to your heart's needs in an *unconscious* way; I certainly did. I made choices that were immature and destructive. One example among many in my life that still makes me cringe is when I "abandoned" my children.

When I lived in San Francisco after my pre-doctoral internship at UCSF, I was in a relationship with someone who lived in Marin, which is about an hour's drive away. My unconscious, desperate need for love, to be with him, was so strong that on most weekends, I left my children to fend for themselves at ages ten and thirteen. Fortunately, my daughter "told" on me to my sisters, and I stopped.

Make no mistake: the heart's cries affect how we live our lives, especially if we ignore them. For that reason alone, it's beneficial to make them as conscious as we can.

"The Dream of the Planet"

In our society, it is easy to get lost in the sirens' song about popularity as teenagers and success as adults, with its attributes of perfect spouse and family, prestige, career, and all the toys. Even toddlers don't escape as their parents often lay down their life tracks early in life. I hear about parents trying to ensure their children's acceptance into Ivy League colleges with the best start in the right prestigious kindergarten.

You learn by example or modeling, through advertising and our culture what it is that you need, not only in your choice of cars or clothes, but in terms of values, lifestyle, and success. Everyone and everything around you program you with the "dream of the planet," (Don Miguel's words, found in *The Four Agreements*). You are rarely encouraged to listen to another drummer or better yet, your own drumbeat.

During my doctoral program in psychology, I faced a horrifying moment when I began my dissertation thesis project. Every idea I could think of was unoriginal. I slowly concluded that I had no original idea in my brain. Up to that time, my entire strategy for success and academic achievement involved absorbing information and articulating it on demand.

In personal relationships, my strategy was to understand the views of others and be careful not to disagree or criticize. I don't know if I could even say that I had an opinion on anything. If I did, I certainly kept it hidden from others as well as from myself.

This is one aspect of the programming, my version of the dream of the planet that dictated my choices. I had adopted a strategy of compliance and a belief about not being important that severely limited my life options—signs of the limited capacities of a child-heart.

It's never too late to start to learn how your feelings inform you about the life that you are currently living. In self-inquiry, ask yourself what would bring you true satisfaction or happiness.

You do best when you are honest with yourself. And remember to consult with your heart, not only your mind.

Because for most of my life I have been deaf to the needs and cries of my heart, I am writing with the hope that you will *care about yourself* in a deeper way, and that you will be *curious about what lies at your core* and begin to listen.

Unusual Cries of the Heart

My own heart carried even deeper wounds from beyond this lifetime. My Japanese-American heritage, with its legacy of the subservience of women, added weight to the beliefs I already carried. I didn't realize that my heart contained not just my own wounds, but those of my ancestors as well. I learned recently that this possibility was verified by recent animal studies showing that DNA carries memories from generation to generation (*Nature Neuroscience*, January 2014). You too might carry the wounds of an ancestral past without even realizing it.

My first emotional explosion occurred in a group process at the Barbara Brennan School of Healing (BBSH) in 2002, where I was learning to be a healer. The common description that we students shared about BBSH was that although most of us chose the school to become healers, we had actually enrolled to be on an express train of self-transformation. One of the elements of the core curriculum was work on our psyche through individual and group sessions.

At one of my class gatherings, I hesitantly indicated that I had an issue to process in front of more than 100 classmates. I had never exposed myself to this rather public experience before in my previous two years, holding to my strategy of being invisible and safe. I surprised myself; it's as if someone pushed me forward.

When I walked into the center of the circle of my peers gathered around me, nothing that came out of my mouth was scripted or in my conscious awareness. I found myself haltingly talking about the legacy of the Japanese women in my lineage who had obediently taken an invisible, silent position in their lives. The accumulated pain and agonies of such bondage came into my body and heart, and I cried uncontrollably with great sobs, my body shaking.

After a few minutes, it was over. I was stunned into silence and wonder. I felt my heart's burden much lighter. I had finally claimed my voice and my truth; this was a moment of triumph.

Another experience continued the thread about my ancestors. I share the full story in Chapter Four. For me, the Child-Heart method has integrated my current and past experiences and my ancestors' agonies. Another piece of my story is a gentle resolution from the wounds from my current life and lineage.

Many times in my life I have experienced the awful pain of feeling imprisoned, which stems from the belief that I can't say no. I truly believed I had no *right* to say no. "No, you can't violate my body." "No, you can't keep hurting me." "No, you can't take away my rights and liberties." Instead, I was compliant, congenial, and accommodating in most relationships, but unhappy in too many sexual encounters.

My young-self believed that terrible consequences would come from saying no. I unconsciously feared I would lose whatever safety, position, and value I had if I said no, especially in the bedroom. But recently I found that through the Child-Heart process, my young-self had healed sufficiently to be able to say no when sex was asked of me. At that moment, it was my truth. No fear was there to stop me.

I now realize what a precious moment it was—my personal prison dissolved . . . and perhaps the end of oppression of centuries ended as well. My young-self needed this final no. My voice and truth were free.

Choosing the Mind as the Authority Is Common

I know too well what happens when your mind is your God. As a child, I heard the message that I should rely on my brain because I didn't have the looks or personality to get ahead in life. Since the message came from my "mom," I took it seriously, and I relied on my intelligence to bring me approval and success as I grew up.

Besides this personal message, our society and its educational institutions stress the importance of the mind and not the heart. Academics leave no room for nurturing emotional intelligence. Consider intelligence tests: you find nothing about emotions but rather what is valued: functions of the intellect in comprehension, analysis, deduction, even with visual-spatial skills.

If you look at what you studied in school and at current offerings, you find subjects stressing the intellect: math, science, history, language arts. In the budget restraints of recent years, the arts and music were the first to go. Even with these "softer" subjects, there is no discussion about how we function as human beings. The study of psychology as an academic subject avoids a productive discussion about how we deal with our emotions.

Where do we learn about love, a most important subject for most of us? Trial and error is how we learn about how to deal with our feelings and how to love. And respect? Compassion? Life purpose? Humility? Community? You won't find those in most school curriculums.

But small changes are occurring.

Recent reports come from teachers and schools that are offering more than the usual. One video shows how a special education teacher greets his students at the beginning of the day with ten minutes of compliments for each child (https://m.youtube.com/watch?v=5ZXNqraH2Og). Students picked up on his acts of kindness and started complimenting each other.

Another recent lengthy and inspiring article (http://ww2.kqed.org/mindshift/2016/03/30/what-changes-when-a-school-embrac

es-mindfulness/) describes how mindfulness programs are spreading in schools, not only for students but also for staff who requested that they be included.

I first learned of programs like these in a 2014 *San Francisco Chronicle* article (http://www.sfgate.com/opinion/open forum/ article/Medita-tion-transforms-roughest-San-Francisco-513 6942. php). The benefits are impressive, with academic performance higher, absenteeism plummeting, fighting and violence decreasing—all because of Quiet Time for ten minutes at the start and end of the school day.

The Child-Heart method uses the power of meditation. Its benefit of creating deep relaxation is the first step in creating the place of imagination. The method bypasses the conscious mind with society's emphasis on logic, analysis, and rationality that most of us use.

In my fifties, something happened that woke me up. I picked up *Autobiography of a Yogi* by Paramahansa Yogananda. By the time I finished the book, I realized my intellect had never given me any answers about how to live my life or how to be happy. Whatever it was in my reading—his spirit or the details that shattered my beliefs about what was possible—my life turned 180 degrees.

In the twenty years since that time, my relationship with my heart has grown slowly. It seems once a major decision like this is made, books, teachers, and adventures come to support the change in direction. All of my teachers in person and through books have expanded my world and my heart beyond what my academic study of psychology gave me. Happily, I've gained momentum as I've focused on the upset two-year-old.

I learned about the two-year-old when I heard my first spiritual teacher, Barbara Johnson of the Open Door community, say, "When you're upset, it's only because you didn't get your way." That teaching has been the key to my study of the two-year-old, and it is a foundational piece in the Child-Heart method.

Especially in this last year, I've grown more sensitive and gained depth. I am experiencing my young-heart—her vulnerability, wounds, and triggers, as well as feeling the prison created by the defenses and strategies used to avoid them. I acknowledged them before with my head but *never felt or lived them*. Now I can hear and feel even small cries of my heart—in any disturbance in my peace.

The Child-Heart Method: A Process to Move Forward

You start by *noticing* the cries and appearance of the two-year-old: upset feelings (like anger or fears), limiting beliefs ("I'm acceptable only if I'm perfect"), strategies ("accomplishment will bring me what I want"), and defenses ("I don't really feel/ see that").

For example: if you are angry or find yourself in a defensive mode, you might be aware enough of what is happening to say, "Oh, it's the two-year-old." This practice of awareness helps build the capacity for witnessing, which is a valuable skill for making changes in your life. For the Child-Heart method, it's the beginning of a relationship with the two-year-old. Sometimes acknowledgement of her is enough to ease the emotional grip of a belief or feeling.

As you assimilate the practices of this method, you will notice the inner child more and more. When your reactions to events or people feel like those of a child, you've probably "found" a young one. For example, when you feel insecure or lack confidence, or feel unreasonable anxiety, you may think, this isn't the adult-me. Yes, it could be the two-year-old. Or if you see yourself trying hard to get someone's approval, you might consider that it's a very "young" strategy.

The Power of the Child-Heart Method

I have doubted myself many times in the past year as I formulated this method. Yet acknowledging the transformations I've witnessed inspire me to move forward. How can I hide what I and others have found?

However, remember that transformation comes at a cost—it means facing your past, which has some hurts you've run or hidden from.

A word of caution: In two different early Child-Heart workshops I conducted, two individuals burst into tears when they suddenly remembered long-forgotten experiences. Both are mature, responsible, competent women with families. Their reaction was a surprise for all.

One never disclosed what she saw, but she said later that it was like having a bandage ripped off a wound she thought had healed. The other remembered a violent event that she apparently preferred to forget. Despite my offers of help, neither chose to revisit their wounds to work on what came up for them.

This disclosure is a warning. The child-selves hide their secrets for a reason. From their *young* perspective, they "judged" the experiences to be overwhelming and unbearable. You may agree *unconsciously* with their assessment.

Episodes like these are clear cries from the heart. If you experience surprising recollections of painful experiences that are overwhelming, please consult a trusted mental health professional.

The Reward of Going Through Your Wounds

This Child-Heart method provides the two-year-old with a corrective experience—fulfilling an important need at the time of wounding. Having someone there for her is essential. The adult is compassionate, kind, and caring. As secrets are exposed, the process allows the adult to see why and how beliefs, defenses, and strategies arose out of the trauma.

Once the heart is unburdened of its hidden content, the limiting beliefs and strategies begin to melt away. The dropping away of the strategies and limiting beliefs allow for new ways of being and creative actions to emerge.

The reward of uncovering your undefended heart, removing the layers of protection, is experiencing its truth, wisdom, vastness, and source in love.

~

QUESTIONS FOR JOURNALING WHEN YOU SIT IN SELF-INQUIRY:

1. What in your daily life is important to you?
2. What nourishes your soul/heart?
3. What gets your full attention in any day? In your life?
4. Describe times in your life when you felt vulnerable, confused, and upset. What did you need? What did you long for?
5. In what ways do you want your life to be better?
6. What is the best life you could dream? What are the obstacles to achieving your dreams?
7. Answer the questions in this chapter that intrigued you.

EXERCISE:

1. Begin, resume, or continue a meditation practice that you've had, or find another one on the Internet. Meditate every day. Start with ten minutes a day for one week. Increase by five minutes the next week. Increase by another five minutes the week after. If you are unfamiliar with meditation, there are beginning meditation tapes available on my website.
2. Check Additional Resources for other suggestions about meditation.

COMMITMENT TO PREPARE FOR YOUR CHILD-HEART SESSION:

1. Practice meditation for a minimum of twenty minutes each day—you can slowly work up to that goal.

2. Commit to at least fifteen minutes a day for journaling—you can start slowly and work up to that goal.

3. Do the exercises at the end of each chapter each week to prepare you for full Child-Heart session.

4. Once you start with the whole Child-Heart method after Chapter Four (after you've done the preparatory exercises in Chapters One through Three), commit to doing one Child-Heart session a week.

[2]

GAINING ACCESS TO THE TWO-YEAR-OLD THROUGH HER TANTRUMS

After participating in a Child-Heart workshop, Sharon described how she saw the senior residents where she worked with new eyes. To her, many were no longer hiding their child-selves. They were throwing tantrums. She asked, "What happened to them as a child to make them so 'crazy' now at 90?"

Once you learn about "adult tantrums," you will probably see many adults showing signs of their inner children in your families and workplaces. Perhaps the perspective that we *all* have wounded hearts will help you develop sympathy for the irritating people in your life.

What about you? There are many cries of the two-year-old that you can potentially see in your everyday life. Yet they are so familiar you accept them as a natural part of your world—just like you rarely question or look at your habits, the source of your emotions, or aspects of your personality.

How the Young Self Calls for Attention

This chapter will help you recognize when the feelings of being upset are coming from your young wounded hearts. It will focus on how upsetting emotions can be used as points of access to your inner child.

Before moving to meet your young-selves using the Child-Heart method, you need to prepare by gathering all signs of your wounded hearts. Why? The more signs you see, the greater your sense of urgency will be to do the Child-Heart work now. Greater awareness of the two-year-old also will sensitize you to recognize more of her persistent calls for your attention. It will seem heartless to ignore her.

The material that follows will help you move closer to that young-self's sobs, pleas, alarms, or whispers. Although you might be tempted to read through the whole chapter without answering the questions posed, please pause to reflect to learn more about yourself.

Gathering Access Points to the Child-Heart

As you go through the following sections in this and the next chapters, record what is meaningful to you—what grabs your attention. Use your journal to gather all the ways you can connect with your young-self to use for your Child-Heart process. You will start with emotions in this chapter, and then move on to a discovery of your beliefs, strategies, and defenses in the next few chapters.

As you do this, you also let the child-parts know of your intention and attention. A Child-Heart session with Diane validated this possibility for me. Diane's young child-self said to her, "I've been watching you. I know now that you've grown up to be a kind person. I can trust you." Because the child-selves are a part of us as adults, it makes sense that they are aware of us as we grow up and live our lives.

Therefore, noticing signs of the child-parts can be a precious prelude to the start of a new kind of relationship with them. Let the inner children know that you are aware of their presence.

When you begin to see and record signs of your child-self, your awareness of her expands: you will gradually find her in the subtlest situations. An example is when I expected my partner to read my mind; I'll share that story in a moment. I'm sure this situation had happened for me before. But only recently after doing Child-Heart work did I become aware of this inner child in this slightly perturbing situation. One more child-self found.

Overreactions and Lingering Emotions
Overreacting to someone's behavior or response to you is a sign of the two-year-old. Here are examples I witnessed recently.

- A retired school principal expressed admiration for how someone had presented a proposal at a recent meeting. She said, "If I were in a similar situation and someone disagreed with me, I'd get upset and start arguing with him."
- A male client was working with someone to keep a dog immobile while performing a procedure on the dog's paw. In his view, neither the dog nor his assistant was cooperating, and he got upset.

The possible child-wound in these instances may be how a lack of control or people disagreeing touched an early sense of "not feeling safe." Or conflict may touch a wound of "not being good/strong/worthy."

Some Child-Heart workshop participants reported feeling angry a lot of the time, especially in response to their husbands or other people around them. One who chose to work with her young-self found one possible source of this anger. At a family gathering when Noni was three years old, an uncle teased her mercilessly for a long time. No one came to stop him or help her. As we spent time with her young-self, we learned from this incident that she felt the shame of feeling unimportant and unvalued.

Who knows how often in her day Noni encounters situations that touch on the wound of "being powerless" or "not being important." It makes sense that when these wounds are touched, she would be upset or angry.

The Emotions that Point to the Young-Self

Below is a list of emotions to help you determine the access points to your two-year-old child-self. It is not a complete list, and you are encouraged to put the feeling in your own words. Your version is the best calling card for the young-self who has these feelings.

When you can see the emotions that are overreactions, that occur when triggered, or that linger, you have your clues. They are clear ways to access the two-year-old.

- Anger, irritation, annoyance, disappointment, frustration
- Resentment, feeling bitter
- Fear, anxiety, worry
- Jealousy, envy
- Sadness and grief
- Feeling guilt, shame, embarrassment
- Feeling helpless, powerless, overwhelmed
- Loneliness
- Abandonment, betrayal
- Feeling confused, lost
- Depression

There are other sources on the Internet that list emotions (one example is http://professional-counselling.com). The list above is no means exhaustive, but includes those that seem most relevant to the Child-Heart method.

Let's review them in detail.

Anger, Irritation, Annoyance, Disappointment, Frustration
Do you get angry in the following situations?

- When in a hurry, you run into long checkout lines or crowded parking lots.
- Trying to clarify suspicious charges on your account with customer care agents, they keep misunderstanding the situation.
- Planning a family event, you hear objections to all your ideas.

In essence, you often run into situations when people and the universe don't "cooperate" with what you want. You may describe your feelings as anger, irritation, disappointment, annoyance, or frustration.

Feeling disturbed momentarily and then letting those feelings pass as you turn to other matters is natural. But if you get intensely or habitually upset and carry this feeling with you through a period of time, it's probably a sign of the two-year-old.

One recent experience involved my annoyance with my partner. We had driven all day to Santa Monica to attend a graduation ceremony. As we were settling into our lodging, we disagreed about a minor thing—the best way to move our suitcases into a hotel room. My irritation persisted, and I could feel myself retreat into my small private world. You would never have guessed how angry I was if you'd seen me spending time with family for three to four hours that evening. The next morning I expected the anger to be gone, but there it was. This is a clear sign of a two-year-old.

Resentment

You can keep your irritation and annoyance hidden. You don't have to express or act out your feelings so others know. When you've held on to unresolved or unexpressed anger for a while, resentment, bitterness, or holding a grudge is a better description. Whether you're still resentful about not being asked decades ago to be part of a bridal party, bitter that you placed second in a poetry competition in high school, or still feeling manipulated into doing something you didn't want to do all point to a child wound.

Fear, Anxiety, and Worry

Anxiety or panic attacks can be hugely uncomfortable and disruptive to normal functioning. Because of a sense of danger, you can feel your body go into alarm, with pulse and heart racing, shallow breathing, feeling jittery and confused, or becoming watchful and ready to take action. The body is preparing for fight or flight.

Extreme anxiety and panic occur in Post-Traumatic Stress Disorder (PTSD), seen clearly in those traumatized by abuse, war, torture—whatever jolts a person out of a sense of safety. Other situations are sexual abuse and violence, where memories are often unavailable but vigilance for threat is high.

Or there can also be quieter moments of internal panic or nervousness. These signs indicate that safety is an issue.

Fears are normal when there is potential danger in a situation. When they come up as an unusual response to a situation in which most would not be afraid, then it's probably a sign of the two-year-old's fears.

Remember that when I use the term "two-year-old," I include all younger versions of child-parts from fetus to adolescent. I met a client's "scraggly" newborn in a Child-Heart session who felt alone, unsupported, and unattended to. In the womb she had been aware of her mother's self-centeredness and indifference to her unborn child. With such early wounding, it's not surprising that the adult reports fear as a major emotional response to many situations. In this case, it's not just fear, but terror because she's very young and without support.

Anxiety may also appear as agitation that distracts you from facing some feeling or thought you don't want. Rather than feeling very angry, for example, an anger-avoidant person might feel anxiety instead. Another Child-Heart client complained about being anxious when she isn't certain about getting the approval she seeks. Rather than facing the fear that she's going to fail, anxiety appears instead.

Worry can be seen as another expression of fear and anxiety, but rather than feeling the emotions, you process them in nonproductive thoughts about the future. You can test this idea for yourself. When you find yourself worrying or expressing your worries, ask yourself, what is it I fear? Of course, many would prefer to worry than feel their fears since worry attempts to control and lessen the intensity of the fear.

Sadness and grief

It is most often with loss of some kind that we feel sadness and grief. Children often experience their first loss when a beloved pet dies.

When leaving for home after a summer full of fun at a lakeside cottage, it's normal to feel sadness. Grief is a stronger emotion that often lasts longer than sadness does. It often occurs when someone close and dear to you is gone.

One of my sisters remarried after the death of her first husband. She was delighted to find another love. However, after six years of marriage, her second husband asked for a divorce. Though it was very hurtful, my sister bore the pain of it well, at least on the surface. One evening as we were making music together she burst into tears while singing "You'll Never Walk Alone." Her tears shocked both of us.

Here is an instance when a two-year-old's buried, unexpressed emotions spilled out. Was it the loneliness she wouldn't admit to herself, or the losses she hadn't cried over, or the disappointment from men in her life that overwhelmed her? When you cry, you might wonder what feelings and needs are unexpressed and hidden in the heart. Without Child-Heart sessions we would not know when my sister's young child-self adopted a strategy of stoicism to keep emotions unexpressed or the hurt of losses hidden in a child-heart.

Jealousy or Envy

Someone is being admired for how they look or how well they did—they received a promotion, became engaged, or their writing was praised by everyone. Are you able to also be appreciative, or do you feel envious, withdraw, get a bit smaller, and feel somewhat devalued?

A Child-Heart workshop participant described how in most aspects of her life she doesn't overreact. However, with her boyfriend she becomes out-of-her-mind jealous when he's paying attention to other women. She knows there is no reason for her to distrust him or his motives, but she can't stop the jealousy—this is a perfect access point to a young-self's heart that holds the pain of rejection or abandonment.

Embarrassment, Humiliation, Feeling Ashamed

Being embarrassed, humiliated, or shamed describe "feeling bad about myself." Someone may have made an innocent comment like "That wasn't a good thing to say," Or "Wow, you really f—ked up." You can smile, say "Oops," perhaps make the correction or apologize, and move on. If some pain or shame continues, it points to a wound.

Feeling vulnerable when you get unwanted attention is a sign of the two-year-old who feels that something is wrong with her. She believes she's defective, unlovable. Or, as reported by a Child-Heart workshop participant, "Shame could come from believing that you are a mistake, inherently flawed, worthless, and having no value. You are nothing but shit. Have no right to be alive."

Have you seen bullies in action? They are masters of the art of humiliation. Their intention is to make victims feel weak and powerless, especially in front of other peers. Many carry these memories and the pain of feeling humiliated—you feel bad about yourself and want to disappear. With shame or humiliation, you believe you did something wrong, or feel accused of being bad or flawed in some way. A bully is able to touch a two-year-old's wound of not being safe or cared for, as well as early beliefs about being wrong.

Regret, Remorse, Guilt

Whether you call it regret, remorse, or guilt, these emotions involve believing that you did something wrong and you feel bad about it. Your conscience bothers you. You've made a mistake that usually involves others. If these feelings linger or come up often, it may a sign of a young child's heart that adopted a belief of being responsible in a difficult time.

"It was my fault." In two Child-Heart sessions with two different individuals, a young child-self came forward to reveal that she believed a family tragedy was her fault. In one situation, the young child was seven years old when her brother died unexpectedly. In the other, a young-self of five years of age responded to her sister's contracting polio in the same way. Both young-selves believed that if it weren't for her, the family tragedy would not have happened.

The guilt they might have felt went into hiding. Instead, they took on the belief that something was their fault, which also went into hiding. The first participant, Lee, adopted the strategy of being very responsible and mature at the age of seven. The second, Lilli, created the strategy of hiding who she was from everyone, as if she wasn't acceptable or worthy of attention.

Incomprehensible as this may seem, the wounded child does the best she can to make sense of her situation. In each of the families, after the death or sudden illness of a child nothing was the same. The usual attention paid to other children changed drastically, as parents attended to the ill child or grieved the death of a son. Each child experienced abandonment. The shock of it and accompanying feelings are the secrets kept safe in the child-heart.

Feeling Helpless, Powerless, Hopeless

As a life rule, I avoid feeling helpless, powerless, and hopeless. It's akin to giving up. Whether you call it my personality, my inborn spirit, or a child-self strategy, I don't give up easily. However, in some situations I've felt immense relief from accepting my feeling of helpless/powerless/hopeless.

I went on a theme park ride where people are securely strapped and secured by bars into their seat. The ride suddenly and rapidly shoots you up about forty feet. As it started, I experienced tensing and fighting through most of the upward projection. Then I gave up. When I did, I laughed, felt relief, and then enjoyed the rest of the ride up and down. The lesson here is that in situations in which I don't have any control or power, I shouldn't struggle against the feelings that arise. A lesson for me in accepting what is.

My two-year-old was tense with fear, not knowing what to expect on this ride. This is similar to the way adults resist change because their young-selves fear the unknown.

Loneliness

Those who complain about feeling lonely fit many descriptions; they are people who:

- live by themselves because they've never partnered with anyone,
- are divorced and whose children have left,
- are without family,
- have lives focused on a physical or emotional disability and are isolated,
- perhaps don't like their own company, or

- live with others but still feel isolated, without an enduring connection with anyone.

Pets, especially dogs, provide a wonderful solution for those who feel lonely. Dogs usually want attention and reciprocate by focusing on you. They greet you when you return home and when you wake up in the morning. You get the constant message *you are important to me.* The loving attention a dog naturally gives qualifies some of them to uplift hospital- or institution-bound individuals. Please take a moment to enjoy this video on the power of puppies at this website http://www.upworthy.com/puppies-invaded-a-retirement-home-preschool-and-gym-pure-bliss-ensued?c=upw1.

Through the example of dogs, you can easily see the need for love and attention that we all have. If you complain of loneliness, perhaps you don't understand how you've protected yourself from people hurting you. You have a wall keeping you safe, but it's also keeping people out. Perhaps you can learn the seeds of it in a child-heart that "chose" emotional isolation.

Abandonment, Betrayal

Many child-wounds come from abandonment by the primary caregiver, who is usually the mother. However long or short the period of time when she stopped her nurturing, the baby felt abandoned and/or betrayed. The safety and comfort felt in one moment was suddenly gone in the next.

Later in life it's natural to feel abandoned or betrayed when a parent, sibling, spouse, love, or best friend leaves or fails to support and nurture you as you need. It may be something minor such as forgetting to show up for a date, or more serious discord that permanently or temporarily ends the relationship. These feelings, and their association to the early wounds we experience, point clearly to the wounded child.

Confusion, Feeling Lost

When you are confused or feeling lost for more than a short time, you may also touch an early wound. The young child once abandoned finds herself in unknown territory with no orientation. If the sense of separation occurred before verbal and cognitive skills developed, there are few resources to aid the abandoned child.

May described what happened to her at age twelve when her mother left to follow a lover to another state. Although she didn't describe feeling confused and lost at the time, her life after that, from ages twelve to fifteen, clearly revealed her confusion. May used alcohol and made desperate attempts to get a boyfriend to fill the loss she felt in her heart. Additional Child-Heart sessions could bring forth a child-self who experienced early abandonment and who may have fears and confusion hidden in her heart.

When people and things that provided you security and safety drop away, such as losing a loved one or your job, profound confusion can set in. It can be a natural part of grief after loss and abandonment.

Depression

It would take a mental health professional to determine whether someone carries the diagnosis of clinical depression. As mentioned in the Introduction, *Listen to the Cries of Your Heart* is not for the treatment of mental and emotional disorders. A discussion of clinical depression is beyond the scope of this book.

When ordinary people say they feel depressed, it takes inquiry to determine exactly what they mean. Here depression is defined as having a low mood; not having the usual energy for living; feeling unengaged with people and activities around them. There is an absence of positive feelings and little motivation to do much.

It's as if a person has given up and lost hope. In analyzing a young child's reaction to severe trauma, giving up is part of the constellation of possible responses. But it's not the main reaction. No one yet has presented with "feeling depressed" as a complaint for Child-Heart work. I repeat this reminder that diagnosable issues such as a presenting complaint of clinical depression is beyond the scope of this book.

Learn Your Heart's Needs from Your Tantrums

When I picture a young child throwing a temper tantrum, I am aware of how the cries cut through whatever ambient noise is present. She is definitely upset. She's not getting what she wants.

When you as an adult are upset, *what is it that you need*? Going deeper still, *what does your heart need*? Recently I saw my two-year-old irritated by my partner's lack of awareness of my needs. I had the child-like expectations that he should "read" my mind or at least acknowledge what was happening for me. A young baby or child expects the same thing: to have mother know what she needs and fulfill those needs for warmth, comfort, food, and nurturing.

A response that shows someone sees my need(s) is one way someone can express love to me. My heart needs someone to know and acknowledge (if not fulfill) my needs. I realize that my adult cannot expect to have her mind read. If I had not taken the time to do some self-inquiry on this incident, I may have concluded that my partner's usual messes were what bothered me. With just a few minutes of pausing to reflect, I found a child-self that wanted the kind of attention a baby might expect—a sign of a wounded heart.

Before a Child-Heart session, a fifteen-year-old described what happened to him when he was eleven and his mother left him for several days for the first time. Her absence created such confusion that the quality of his work at school plummeted. On the next trip away, his mother prepared him by explaining more fully what she would be doing while away and by arranging for Skype calls with him.

Before his obvious confusion and despair after his mother left, there had been no sign of a wounded heart. His mother had no way of knowing that his child-heart believed that if she wasn't physically present, her love for him disappeared.

Earlier we met Noni, who was angry at a family gathering about her uncle's teasing. This young child-self *needed to be important enough* for someone to stand up for her. She *needed her uncle to take her seriously* so he'd stop what he was doing. She *needed someone to care* in those moments about how she felt. In a Child-Heart session she has the opportunity to feel these needs in her child-heart.

Love in its many expressions is a fundamental need for most of us. Not having the love we need may be the reason for all of our upsets.

How to Learn Your Heart's Needs or Longings

Through the years, I've learned about my needs and longings through reflection or self-inquiry. After teaching college-level philosophy classes for eight years, I turned the Socratic method used with students on myself: Where was my life headed? I realized that I didn't want to continue to teach "forever." Then, for the first time I asked what my needs were if I wanted to make a change. The answer: I wanted to go back to college and do it "right."

That was the beginning of my seven-year trek to a PhD. Had I not bothered to ask myself questions, I wonder where I would be today. No doubt my life would be vastly different.

I recommend self-inquiry as a way of uncovering what your heart needs and longs for.

Learning about Your Needs through the Child-Heart Method

Some of us can use the questions above to reach deep into our hearts to discover what we truly need and yearn for. For others, it takes time to get there. No matter. Patience is important to practice for our lives and especially for the Child-Heart process.

Although our self-inquiry may yield answers to these questions, sometimes they seem more from the mind than from the heart. The Child-Heart process allows you to experience the needs in a different way: you feel them.

This chapter guides you to notice and take seriously your negative emotions, especially those that call out with intensity, frequency, or persistence. Emotions are responses of your heart. They can be your emotional "thermometer," telling you how healthy your life is. When you spend time with your feelings in self-inquiry and in the Child-Heart process, you learn what you need to be fulfilled. You will gain clarity and purpose in your life.

Once you have identified at least one upsetting feeling that points to a child-self, you are ready for an understanding of the Child-Heart method in the next chapter.

∾

JOURNALING QUESTIONS:
1. Sitting with the list of emotions above, choose the three that are most disturbing to you.
2. With each emotions describe the circumstances in which they arise and the details of how you feel and what you think. In each case, what do you need?
3. Look at times that you have been upset; describe the situation and what you did.
4. When you are upset, what does your heart need?

EXERCISE: CREATING A PLACE OF SAFETY
1. Think back through your past to find a safe place, or create one with your imagination, including all elements that convey safety. These elements might include a mountain or meadow setting, ocean, lakes, streams, trees, a cave, animals,

birds, boulders, the night sky—anything that makes you feel safe.

2. A recording is available to guide you through this process on my website.

[3]

DETAILS OF THE CHILD-HEART METHOD

The purpose in writing this book was to put together enough information and guidance so that *committed individuals could conduct themselves through Child-Heart sessions.* Especially by using the recordings that I've made (you'll find them on my website), you can begin to interact with your child-selves.

The Child-Heart Protocol

In the following pages, you will learn more about the components of the method as well as other information that will deepen your understanding of what is involved.

Let's review the ten components of the method:

1. **Create a Safe Place of the Imagination.** Achieving deep relaxation is an important first step. If you are unfamiliar with how to do this, you will find a recording guiding you to deep relaxation and to creating a safe place at my website.

   Start breathing deeply with your eyes closed. Watch your breath as it moves in and out. With each succeeding breath you will relax even more. On the exhale, notice any tension in your muscles, and let go. Breathing in, appreciate oxygen that Mother Earth consistently and freely provides to support life in your body. Breathing out, let go of tension and whatever doesn't serve you. As you move more deeply into relaxation you are in the world where the veil between conscious and less conscious is thin. There is no time; all memory is present. *Bring in your place of safety,* either real or imagined.

2. **Name what is most sacred to you right now.** What is sacred brings a larger sense of safety than we ordinarily feel. By evoking the sacred, we also bring a higher vibration and support into the space.

3. **Be present and invite a young-self to appear.** She holds the secrets about this particular emotion. You may have to wait patiently for her appearance.

4. **Imagine a young-self stepping forward.** If one doesn't appear, in your imagination go through photos of when you were young, and pick one of them to use.

5. **Thank and welcome her for showing up.** Tell her you are grateful for the opportunity to know the young-self, to begin a healing, and especially for her holding the difficult feelings after a trauma.

6. **Picture standing in front of the child.** See what you can in her posture, her face, her eyes, and eventually sense deeply *into her heart.* Make yourself visible to her.

7. **Listen with curiosity.** You might ask the child (either out loud or in your mind) what she's feeling and experiencing. Or reflect back what you see. When you describe what you sense about her, she has the opportunity to get a better sense of you. If you can tell how old she is, you might remember what might have been going on in her life at that time.

8. **Accept your child-self.** Let her know it is okay to feel what she feels. Imagine looking into her eyes with acknowledgement and compassion. Or just be there with silent acceptance, especially of what she reveals from her heart.

9. **Offer her attention and compassion.** Remember that she's been alone ever since her "trauma" of separation. If she accepts or even enjoys your presence, it's an important change. When she talks about how she sees things, you the adult can

"correct" her reality with messages like "You are okay," or "You didn't feel loved, not because you're bad but your parents couldn't provide the love you needed."

10. **Commit to return to her,** especially if you feel that she needs more time to trust you, or if she's shared some of her experiences but you sense her sharing is incomplete. Or commit to return to interact with other child-selves.

Essential Components of the Child-Heart Method

In this chapter, you will learn the basics of the Child-Heart method for accessing your child-selves and integrating them. Each step of the Child-Heart Method is important. However, there are some ingredients that I consider essential: the place of imagination, the sense of safety, using what is most sacred right now, appreciation, being present, compassion, curiosity, patience, and a felt connection that ends the sense of being alone. We will discuss each of these essential ingredients now and then put them together in an actual session through your exercise assignment at the end of the next chapter.

The Place of Imagination

The most direct way to facilitate deep changes with issues rooted in the heart is to work in a place that has access to the subconscious, what I call the imaginal space, or the place of imagination.

How Deep Relaxation Is Used to Access to the Imaginal Space

Those who practice meditation are familiar with a deeply relaxed state. Dr. Brian Weiss, a psychiatrist specializing in past-life regressions, uses the technique of deep relaxation and creating a garden of safety to begin his past-life regression process. In this space, individuals can access their lives in the past.

Meditators often describe altered states of consciousness during meditation. Meditation practice is therefore helpful for better access to the imaginal place, which is the context of Child-Heart work.

Within the imaginal space in the Child-Heart Method, the adult invites a child-self to appear and moves to be in her presence. Interactions occur that have impact on both child-self and adult-self.

Visualization techniques use this place of imagination to create change. Hypnosis accesses this place to implant suggestions for needed changes in behavior and perspective. Shamans use drumming to induce the same state to guide listeners on their shamanic journeys. Others such as Richard Bartlett of Matrix Energetics and Robert Moss of Quantum Dreaming use the quantum space verified by recent physics to create "miracles." This imaginal space is a quantum space where all possibilities exist where an adult can move back into the past to meet child-selves.

It is a place where spending time with your young-selves can have experiences that make a difference to both adult and child.

A Place or Space of Safety

Early hurts impacted the young child with a message that the world isn't safe, that it is not a friendly place. Before interacting with her, creating safety in the imaginal place is important. If you have in your history a favorite place that made you feel safe, you can use that as an anchor. Or you can create a place in your imagination by including elements that feel special to you.

Sometimes a participant reports, "Nothing is happening." "My mind is drifting." "I'm bored." Or even, "I'm getting sleepy." I interpret these reports as resistance in either adult or child. When this occurs before or during the interaction, safety or fear is usually the issue. When this happens, I suggest the adult remember her safe place.

What Is Most Sacred Right Now

Another aspect of creating the best context for the child-heart process is adding the name of what is most sacred to the imaginal space. When creating the imaginal place, I ask the adult to say out loud the name of what is most sacred at the moment. It could be a symbol like infinity, or Nature, Beauty, Kwan Yin, St. Francis, the Christ, the I-Am, Buddha—whatever evokes awe and wonder, whatever feels supportive and protective.

Those who have some spiritual practice and believe in the power of unseen forces are more likely to feel supported by spirits, angels, or divine beings. Also those who can feel something more than obvious reality—for example, awe in Nature's displays—can add to this imaginal space with such experiences. The ocean, a sunset, a stream, the forest, a river, a meadow, a bird or flower, the sky or clouds are all possibilities.

Naming what is most sacred adds greater safety to the imaginal place. What is sacred usually connects the adult to some "reality" greater than her usual reality, one that the adult touches in awe, wonder, or stillness. The sacred brings in a different quality of safety.

Being Present

Being present to the child without the adult's agenda is not easy. For most of us, what grabs our attention is doing rather than being. Our ability to stay present can increase through a meditation practice. When we can be present, we forget our self—self-forgetting.

You have many more moments of "being present" than you realize. Whenever you are captured by the spirit or beauty of a piece of art, architecture, or sculpture, or when your heart soars with music; when you forget time staring at a rose or a stream; when a baby's innocent eyes gaze at you; when you are awed by whatever you're focusing on—these are moments of self-forgetting and being present.

Expressing Appreciation

When I guide someone through the Child-Heart method, I remember to say *thank you* often—especially to the young-self who shows up. When she begins to show what's in her heart, I *feel* and express appreciation. Appreciation of each part of our personalities, including our child-selves—our strategies, defenses, beliefs—fosters trust, integration, and the connection necessary for corrective experiences.

Decades ago, when I first began inner child work, I learned the impact and power of appreciation. Because my first client experienced violent and cruel physical abuse in early childhood, monsters lined the internal path to the child-self. It took repeated sessions going within before the monsters no longer prevented passage.

Sufficient conversations and connections occurred with the young-self so that the monsters lost their purpose and felt they had no place to be. They didn't want to leave their home. However, once I acknowledged their protective roles and that they still had a role to play to protect the adult client from real threats, they were relieved. They no longer had their monster appearance to the client because they were respectfully acknowledged and appreciated.

Compassion

There must be thousands—if not millions—of words written about compassion. You might have read some. For now, let me just remind you of the Latin root of the word: *com* is together, *to be with*, and *passion* refers to suffering.

Having compassion is to be present with the suffering or feelings of others. It is not to superimpose your understanding or your feelings on them; not to rescue or fix them; not to empathize and feel their feelings. The adult has the opportunity to be with those feelings: *to be separate yet present*. Practice building your compassion "muscle" if it's weak.

Sometimes it's easy to have empathy and feel the child-self's feelings within us. It's important to learn about the feelings in the child-heart but not to retain those feelings within us. In order to have compassion for the child-self you may have to "give" them back to her to maintain your adult grounded-ness.

If you have questions about whose feelings you have, check to see how grounded or solid you are. You may find it helpful to locate the feeling in your body and ask how old are you? You then learn the reason your compassion hasn't affected the child: you are holding her feelings for her.

Gratitude

Whenever the flow of interaction between child-self and adult isn't moving smoothly, I'm prompted to modify the protocol when I act as a Child-Heart guide. I add to the protocol whenever I see that the child-self is holding back or displaying a lack of trust. Along with compassion, gratitude is also expressed for the role the child-self has played to provide the protection needed for growing up.

These two states of gratitude and appreciation have a higher vibration (that is, I and most people feel more energy or more alive in these states), which catalyzes the Child-Heart process.

You can experiment with these higher vibrations when you compare how you feel when saying certain words. As an experiment, say the word *hate* or *cruel* and then the word *thank you* or *kindness*, and note the difference in how you feel.

The work of Dr. Masaru Emoto, who studied the effect of words on water molecules, is relevant here. His photographs of frozen water molecules show dramatic differences when a word such as *love* is placed next to a beaker of water compared with words like *war* or *anger.*

When you say or think words of gratitude and compassion, a similar result purportedly occurs in your body, which is at least 65 percent water.

The practice of Self-Identity Ho-o-ponopono, discussed by Ihaleakela Hew Len, PhD, and Joe Vitale in their book *Zero Limits*, illustrates the power of words like I love you, thank you, and I forgive you. Joe Vitale wrote a post for his blog, www.mrfire.com titled, "The World's Most Unusual Therapist," in which he described how Dr. Hew Lew changed the conditions and people at a Hawaii state hospital for the criminally insane within weeks of his hire as a staff psychologist.

He never saw any of the inmates, but sat in his office with their thick files. For every disturbing negative event he saw, Dr. Hew Len expressed gratitude and love. He interpreted what seemed negative to him as a call from his own child-part who had a memory associated with that issue. (In the Self-Identity Ho-oponopono system, when an adult sees a negative event it is related to the child of his past who is holding a memory that needs releasing.) The transformations that occurred in the hospital were incredible.

Curiosity

Being curious is opening yourself to the unknown and to the possibilities in a new situation. You move away from the fixed idea of what is before you. You pay attention to details you may have previously disregarded. Everything is important. This is how young children respond to their environment. They haven't created fixed filters and ideas of how things are. They look at the entire world around them.

Curiosity is another form of self-forgetting when the self is full of constructs, judgments and needing to be right. Be curious, open-minded, and openhearted as you stand as witness before the child-self and her heart.

Patience

Being patient comes with having no agenda but instead attending to all the details before you. It's about waiting for what unfolds. In the Child-Heart process, the child-self may not yet trust enough in your commitment or capacity to be with her. She has a tenacious hold of the defenses and strategies created to keep the young heart safe. She may not be willing to give the protection up easily. For the adult, patience is about appreciating what is going on for her and waiting, and possibly returning for more meetings and conversations. The interaction is about her and for her, not about or for the adult. Having patience is another type of self-forgetting.

A Felt Connection

In a Child-Heart interaction, the child-self shifts from isolation and hanging on to intense negative feelings to feeling known, seen, and cared about. Both adult and child-self may experience relief and feel a shift simultaneously.

This compassionate connection is essential; without it, the child probably won't experience any difference. The change in the child-self is evidence of compassion being experienced. When it doesn't occur, it may be because she has yet to fully experience a witnessing, acceptance, and connection about all of her heart's secrets.

Some child-selves may shield themselves so they cannot feel the compassion and presence of the adult at first. It may take repeated connections until they open to what the adult offers.

Be watchful for signs in the adult or the child that a connection occurs. Sometimes the child starts to cry or relaxes, or a "melting" occurs that the adult can feel. Some participants have described this melting as a merging of the child-self with the adult-self.

Some Child-Heart participants impulsively reach out and hold the child, often placing her in the adult's lap. It's a natural impulse to comfort. However, that may not always be the corrective experience sought. It's best to move as deeply as you can into the child's heart by expressing compassion for what has been revealed and asking for what else is being held secret.

A Conscious Commitment

Before you start using the Child-Heart protocol, it's important to be clear about your commitment to your well-being and the well-being of your "lost children." Only a strong dedication to do this work will keep you on course so you aren't swallowed up by the distractions in your usual life. If you start and stop, your lost children remain lost, isolated, and abandoned, wanting to come home. They are alone again.

One workshop participant, after she made contact with her first child-self, committed to building a relationship to connect with all child-parts. Her spirit touches my heart; here is her story.

After our time together, I felt slightly raw, but mostly I felt that I'd met myself for the first time. The process was utterly honest and thought provoking. To be honest, I've been avoiding my inner child. Why? Maybe I was afraid of her. Maybe I was worried about what she might tell me or reveal to me. Maybe I felt guilty that I let her down because there were so many times I was not allowing her to be herself . . . as if I was telling her to be what everyone expected her to be. I was ashamed of her heart, her openness, her willingness to help, her seriousness.

During the (Child-Heart) process, I finally made myself face her and watch her experience all of the hurts and wants. In turn, it gave me the chance to embrace her and tell her I was sorry for not allowing her to be her true self. I told her not to change, to honor her and the honesty that comes with being her true self. I want her to be proud of her willingness to help, be honest, loving, without expectations from others . . . just be her true self. I know that because I have not honored my inner child, I have learned not to be honest and true to myself in adulthood. I'm constantly worried about what others think about what I feel most passionate about. This is a journey of discovery and renewal, and although I'm scared and hesitant, I'm ready.

If you operate as I do, enrolling in a class helps with getting through study material such as these Child-Heart chapters and exercises. You can shore up your commitment to your well-being and your child-selves by joining me in six weekly classes or three weekly workshops through conference calls or webinars.

Happiness as an Access Point to Connect with a Young-Self
Through the exercises that I've provided at the end of the earlier chapters, you have made yourself comfortable with the process of moving into deep relaxation and then moving into the imaginal space. Instructions were provided earlier and recordings to guide you are available on my website. By doing the exercises at the bottom of each of the last two chapters, you've practiced making the space safe or imagining a scene that makes you feel most safe. After taking these steps, you are ready to learn the next steps.

To become familiar with the Child-Heart protocol, it's best and easiest to start by contacting a happy young child. Once a child appears, you notice everything about her—physical and emotional details and her age. The next step is making your presence known by imagining yourself stepping in front of or next to her. If she's shy, she may not be ready for contact. You notice that and give her time to get used to your presence.

You might express appreciation for what you see in her—that might be the joy, spirit, carefree attitude, or the love of play you see in her. Then thank her for showing up and spending time with you.

Using this first venture to move backward in time will accustom you to how the process unfolds. It also provides a chance to be with a younger you who may be expressing herself in ways that you've forgotten. Giving the young-self a chance to hear your positive regard for her may also be very helpful. After all, how often did she get such full attention in her young life?

Child-Heart Process to Find a Happy Child

In recent Child-Heart workshops, we used the process described above to find a happy child. Below are reports from these participants.

The following comes from a gentle man in his early sixties who retired after a full career as a health professional. He describes his early childhood as full of turmoil and trauma.

> *[I'm] hanging out in a gingko tree with a friend of mine, and just being aware of laughing; no troubles, no worries . . . feeling connected with a friend. [This scene] morphed into fourth grade when I have a friendship with one of the students. I just remember it, I don't think I ever acknowledged it . . . how important, how connected we were. . . the thing about the memory was that I never took in how connected we were.*

Given his often-challenging childhood experiences, it was lovely to learn that he found a happy, carefree child. In contrast with that mostly unhappy childhood the following response of mixed emotions came from an almost-retired teacher of the arts. This respondent is almost always smiling and endlessly optimistic.

> *We had a bright backyard . . . we grew up in Montana . . . lots of memories . . . I saw myself standing in front of this tall fence when my boyfriend was on the other side; he was two years old; it was so much fun looking. I won a contest and won a cowgirl outfit. . . . I had to pose . . . remembering it's about pleasing others.*

Yet in this pleasant memory, there is already a hint of the results of a wounded heart.

A sunny and bubbly disposition also describes the following workshop participant—a successful, innovative mental health professional in her forties who works with teenagers.

> *I was about five years old, lived in Santa Monica, the beach was my backyard . . . a creek running into the sea . . . a sacred spot in Native American tradition . . . image of being at that beach, so intent on dripping sand castles . . . so in Nature, it was holding me, almost observing me . . . almost loving me, like saying "I love this little girl."*

This participant clearly found a happy child who felt seen and held by Nature. The joy she felt was contagious—the purpose of the exercise was fulfilled.

In contrast to how most workshop participants came into the Child-Heart workshop space, the following mother of three children was clearly upset. Tears flowed for most of the time we spent together, until she found a child-self and felt relief.

> *I have a hard time remembering one . . . there must be a happy time . . . I was four when my parents divorced. I was . . . laughing, bouncing . . . when I see my kids doing that, I say, yes, that was me. . . . I've smushed the little girl so far down.*

Usually Child-Heart workshop participants seem comfortable moving toward a happy young-self, and they express surprise at the results. Many are grateful to remember a happy childhood time. I remember their beaming, grateful faces.

Negative Emotions or Situations as Access Points
Once you have found a happy child, the next step is to access the not-so-happy parts. As I mentioned before, the easiest way

to access the two-year-old is by focusing on a disturbing feeling in a recent incident or something felt chronically such as fear, anxiety, sadness, shame, or anger. To help them get started, I have Child-Heart workshop participants review a list similar to the one you examined in the previous chapter.

Examples below come from the same workshop participants described earlier in this chapter. They examined the list and shared their "top" emotions. Their actual words may give you a sense of how important and impactful those emotions are.

The tearful mother of three said:

>*Anxiety. I'm a failure . . . I . . . recently ended a relationship . . . I have so much anxiety that I was too much . . . I didn't know how much of it I was carrying around until I ended it . . . like letting out the pressure relief valve.*

The bright, bubbly woman in her forties, who found a lovely young-self at the beach:

>*Jealousy. It's so strange to me. I turn into some . . . a Medusa character. I don't know where it comes from, and I don't understand it. That's a wound right there . . . I think that with my partner, he's charismatic and he can be flirtatious and it doesn't mean anything . . . I lose it.*

The workshop participant who found her happy child in Montana (where a hint of a wounding was included), expressed her feelings more fully about what troubled her.

>*Fear and anxiety. . . . If I get criticism, I feel like I'm not enough. But I think my fear and anxiety permeate everything about me because it's a fear about not being better than I am . . . As a child, I had to be the best . . . felt I couldn't be (anything but) that.*

A common experience in these Child-Heart workshops is participants responding to others by saying, "I feel that way too." Some have said, "Ditto for me on everything everyone has said."

I hope you find it comforting to hear that you are not alone in how you feel.

Beginning the Child-Heart Method by Building Rapport

Once you are comfortable with the process of journeying to the place of imagination and spending time with a young self, the next step is to invite a child-self connected to an emotion to join you or whatever child-part is most eager to be with you.

In engaging with a child-self, all your people skills are required. Your intention is to build rapport, especially if she seems shy or reluctant to make contact. To develop rapport, you can express appreciation for all you can see and sense about the child-self. Remember that you are with a hurt child-self—you may have to proceed slowly until she becomes comfortable with you.

It is helpful to express compassion for what she's feeling as well as how much you appreciate that she's been keeping painful reactions secret to protect you.

When the child-self is comfortable with your presence, you can ask what she holds in the heart. Invite her to share what she can. To get her started, you might express what you imagine is there and wait for confirmation. Notice if there are changes in her as she reveals more and as she hears from you. When appropriate, include these questions in your dialogue:

- Do you hold secrets in your heart?
- Will you share some of your secrets with me?
- What do you need?
- What can I do for you?

Hopefully, when the child hears expressions of compassion and appreciation and senses your curiosity and concern, she reveals more. She learns she doesn't have to be alone with what weighs heavily in her heart.

As you move to witnessing the secrets in the heart and the painful results of the trauma, be in your compassionate heart. Articulating the ways a child-self has coped begins to deepen the adult's sensitivity and compassion for what the child-heart holds. If there isn't an easy flow in the session (the child-self is not moving or interacting), I articulate what could be happening for the child-self. You might say things out loud or in your mind in response to what she's shown you, such as "That seems hard," or "I'm sorry." Watch for changes as she reveals what she can.

I might also say some parts of the following that I've used in different sessions:

- After the *shock* of having safety and comfort suddenly disappear
- There must be *bewilderment, confusion, and/or fear* in sensing being alone
- *Anger* for being left
- A struggle to keep from *giving up*
- Even feeling *self-destructive*
- Not knowing what to do, feeling *helpless*
- Like being taken from light and comfort to darkness and *distress*
- Having something comforting and warm *ripped* away
- Falling into a *black* hole
- Feeling searing *pain*

It's important to be patient, to give her enough time with you for your presence to interrupt her aloneness. Respond to her beliefs that she is at fault or is bad. Give her a broader perspective to let her know that she didn't get what she needed and it was not her fault. Communicate with her long enough so that your presence and words affect her.

There may also be intermediate stages before a corrective connection happens. You may learn from the child-self about a belief formed at the time of wounding: "I am alone." "No one is here for me." "I can't expect anyone to help me." "I'm not okay." You can respond by saying: "Yes, you were alone but now I am here with you." "I am here to help you in whatever way I can." "Given what you experienced, it's easy to conclude that you're not okay. But that's not the truth. You are okay."

Stopping at the intermediate stage is often enough for one Child-Heart session. The adult may feel relief, even a sense of freedom because the child has accepted "You're okay," "It's not your fault," "You're not alone; I'm here with you."

To end the session, thank her for showing up, for having the courage and spirit to step forward; thank her for the trust in you that she showed in connecting with you. If you sense that your time together wasn't complete because she holds more secrets, then promise that you will return to spend time with her again. And you can commit to returning to interact with other child-selves.

When I guide someone through a Child-Heart session, the adult usually says it's time to end. Or I sense an end that usually happens when a child-self has expressed a need (such as to play) that is met, a belief the adult has responded to with the truth, or signs of transformation apparent in the child-self.

Gently move away from the scene and begin to pay attention to your breathing. After you follow a few breaths in and out, slowly open your eyes when ready.

Write an entry in your journal about what you discovered before details fade.

The Completion of the Child-Heart Process

In a recent Child-Heart workshop, "Diane" went through two amazing sessions in a group process as well as an individual process in a two-hour period. The transformation she experienced highlights and clarifies when the Child-Heart process is complete.

Diane described how she has been to fifty therapists in her adult life, looking for a solution or resolution to the difficult experiences of her childhood. Diane also meditated and used other spiritual practices to find peace. Yet there were few days in her life that she didn't awaken with terror—a terror that kept her in bed every morning for at least twenty minutes before she felt steady enough to get out of bed.

In her first session, she encountered a very angry young-self. She was angry especially with her mother because mother "talked her out of" her judgment about an uncle. Diane did not like him and didn't want anything to do with him, but she relented under pressure from her parents. When she allowed his presence, that uncle sexually molested her in a violent manner.

Her young-heart revealed overwhelming anger, and the child didn't believe she could handle it. It's common for young child-selves to judge intense feelings of anger, fear, or desperation as overwhelming and too painful to bear. With the security provided by the adult, and the place of safety Diane called on, she felt safe. The child fully revealed her hidden anger to the adult, and with that she freed herself. With the compassionate presence of the adult, the young-heart no longer needed to keep it secret. Both the young child and the adult felt the release.

After the session, Diane said, "I'm not the same person who walked into this room earlier in the day. I feel different."

Diane's second session involved finding the young child locked in a "dark, scary place" by her father. She was frantic; she didn't understand why she was there. She cried out for help, but she finally gave up and fell asleep. When Diane contacted the young-self, the difficult reactions to this event were articulated, seen, and acknowledged. Still, the young child refused to be comforted.

When I joined in with appreciation of her mistrust and her need to keep herself safe, and expressed compassion for her, she responded by saying, "Can I tell you more?" Then she explained what had happened before she ended up in the closet—how when she went outside to play, her father had asked her whether she was cold and needed a sweater. She said no. He asked again and again. She kept saying what was true for her: "No, I'm not cold, so why do I need a sweater?" He suddenly grabbed her in rage, shook her, and threw her in the "dark, scary place."

Once the secret was out of her heart, she accepted the gratitude, appreciation, and compassion expressed by both of us. The young child-self asked for holding, and then "melted" (the adult Diane's word) in an embrace with her adult-self.

The next morning, Diane did not experience the usual terror. Instead, she felt just hints of it, along with the recognition that she could bring in "her safe place." She reported how she used her awareness of choice: she could either decide to move away from the feelings that had gripped her for decades, or feel the safety she could remember. Later in the day when Diane was walking in a familiar place, she realized she was seeing the world differently; "There are more spaces between leaves and branches" was her description.

Other Transformations through the Child-Heart Process

When the Child-Heart process is complete, the child-self changes in appearance and in emotions. Adult participants have reported, "She's drinking in the love; she's ecstatic." "The baby became a one-year-old." "She's comforted and feels safe." These statements, often accompanied by a sense of awe, were possible because the child-self could take in messages like "You're never alone" or "You're okay" or "It isn't your fault." When asked if the child-self was reassured, the responses included, "Yes, she can take a deep breath." "She has a peaceful face . . . all lit up, soft . . . trusting . . . she feels at home."

Sometimes confirmation comes in the form of light. Light fills the child-self and/or the whole scene providing further confirmation. Some examples of connection being made are: "I'm this vast (sphere) of golden light, overwhelming all senses at the moment." "I get to bring home this girl. She's just pure light."

Although it's satisfying to have a Child-Heart process move to completion and transformation, it isn't necessary. Whatever time spent with a young-self is part of building a relationship with her. The adult can return anytime to resume the process to learn more about the secrets held in the child-heart.

Using the Child-Heart Method on Your Own

You now have the information and resources to use the Child-Heart method on your own. You've prepared for this experience by first practicing deep relaxation, creating an imaginal place, and providing safety within that place. You've read through an extensive explanation of the procedure.

At this juncture, you may want to take the time to guide your own Child-Heart sessions for yourself, at least to find a happy child. However, please remember: If you don't want to work on your own, or if you run into difficulties while doing this work on your own, you are welcome to reach out for my services. An additional witness/compassionate presence in the process can be helpful to both child and adult.

Some of you may want to have your first Child-Heart sessions guided by me. I welcome the opportunity to work with you one-on-one. For others, I recommend that you enroll either in workshops or in classes that I provide.

If you are already in counseling or psychotherapy, I suggest you inquire with your practitioner about the possibility of doing Child-Heart work in your sessions. My website includes a special section for counselors and therapists who are open to expanding their offerings. Access to this material will be provided to interested counselors only after consultation with me.

The next chapter with its edited transcripts can bring to life Child-Heart sessions for which you've only received instructions. They may leave you better prepared to try one on your own.

Blessings on whatever choice you make.

∼

JOURNALING QUESTIONS:

1. What can you do to stay committed to connecting with your child-selves?
2. Search for experiences when you were "present" to what was before you, and when someone else was "present" to you, compassionate with you. Describe how you felt.

EXERCISE:

1. Complete at least one Child-Heart session to meet a happy child (usually short and serves as a taste of a Child-Heart session).
2. Complete at least one Child-Heart session starting with an upsetting emotion.
3. Join a Child-Heart class or workshop that will include being led through one session as a group. Details are found on my website.
4. Remember that there are recordings for guidance for these assignments on my website.

[4]

SAMPLES OF FULL CHILD-HEART SESSIONS

Edited transcripts of Child-Heart sessions below provide examples of how the protocol works. Some are straightforward. Others seem to move off track. When you read through transcripts of Child-Heart sessions, you can appreciate the vulnerability apparent in the participants and the differences that make each one unique.

A Complete Child-Heart Process

The following Child-Heart session is with an individual who is very conscientious in evolving to the highest level of maturation and awakening. Lilli is married, with three adult children and a grandchild. She has extensive training in a number of healing practices. Currently, she works comfortably and confidently as a shamanic healer. Though Lilli has done much personal work, she still has some areas of difficulties. She happily volunteered to use the Child-Heart method.

[Plain font is the gist of my guidance; client responses are in *italics*.]

"Recall . . . the most intense feelings you have about being stuck here. Not finding the answers. How that made you feel."

"Incredibly frustrated."

"Now we're going to invite and call forth a child-part that knows this situation well or knows something about this twelve-year long battle [a health issue] to come forward at this time."

"A little girl. She's about three or four."

"How does she look to you?"

"Like a photo of myself I used to see . . . a little girl with a curly mop of white hair."

"What's her stance? Her facial expression?"

"She's full of mischief. Yeah, she got a lot of bounce in her."

"Thank you for showing up. So it's beautiful when you remember a child part of you that has innocence, that mischief, that energy. . . . And we're going to ask this child part if there is an early part of her, or later part of her, that experienced something that was hurtful."

"What immediately comes to mind . . . and what always comes to mind when I make inquiries is a baby in the cradle, and her arms, hands are up. She's waving her hands. . . . It's for attention . . . she's wants attention."

"And it hasn't come. Now see her, a little longer, watching her . . . and see what happens in the minutes beyond that or the minutes before that."

"She's crying . . . minutes before . . . what's coming to my mind: she needs her mother's undivided attention."

"And when it wasn't there . . . can you see what happened in her heart?"

"What I'm seeing is her heart breaking in two."

"Can you allow yourself to know what that felt like?"

"I can already feel it. I'm starting to cry."

"While it's okay to cry, what is important is for you to know and understand. So let's both of us be with her as her heart is breaking and the pain that comes forth and whatever else happens . . . notice other feelings, other efforts, other energies accompanying this event."

"I feel anger . . . a lot of anger . . . very angry about it . . . confusion and anger, not understanding why this has happened, but she's angry too for this happening."

"I can imagine in some way before moments like this happen that we're all very comfortable, such as experiencing in the womb all our needs taken care of. But an interruption of this happens, and it's such a shock that we have no orientation, we are lost, we are confused. 'Somebody out there. Mom, mother . . . where are you?' And no response . . . more pain, frustration, confusion, bewildered, afraid . . . any sense of fear?"

"I'm getting a sense of rage that I've been put into this situation . . . and I want to go back where it's safe . . . before being born . . . why was I born into this place? I don't want to be here."

"Thank you."

[Shortly after this, a shift happens.]

"Yeah . . . (long pause) I'm actually beginning to feel the energy in my body . . . my arms, my heart . . . all over."

"Can that child's heart really take in the energy of the Ground-of-Being [what was most sacred to the adult], the energy of love?"

"I pick her up and hold her . . . and yes, I think she can take it [in] . . . She can feel safe."

"Check in with her . . . see if being with you and what you've been experiencing with her has an effect on her heart."

"Feels like it did . . . I see green energy in her heart . . . green to me is . . . the energy of the heart chakra, of love, energy of growth, of Nature." [Long pause]

"How is the baby's heart doing?"

"Well, it's like she's gotten bigger; she's sat up and has her arms around my neck. She's smiling . . . I see this golden light going through her hair. She's happy; she's laughing."

Commentary

This session follows the Child-Heart protocol of starting with an invitation, a description of the child part who appears, being present to what is distressing for her with the adult's love and compassion, and seeing the transformation in the child—her growing up a bit more. Notice how the guidance focused on revealing more than one emotion.

In this session conducted early in my time with the Child-Heart method, I wasn't insisting on how the adult knew the feelings of the child-self. Lilli apparently had the feelings herself. By exploring what was in the child-heart, she knew more of the distress of the young-self. How she knew and held these feelings didn't interfere with the compassionate connection created. The connection between them was sufficient for a corrective experience for the young self.

Child-Heart Session with the Baby in Utero

The next edited transcript is a session with a mother of two who has done other inner-child work as well as other healing work before attending a Child-Heart workshop. We are in a Reiki meditation group together. In recent years she's had all the turmoil and challenges that divorce brings. She's well aware of her issues and conscientious about resolving them and moving forward to her life of service. This was her follow-up session. She arrived with possible child-selves she was aware of to invite.

"Find a child-self with something in her heart she's held secret from you . . . either . . . a seven-year-old or baby in utero."
"The newborn . . . it's actually in utero, all curled up. [sigh]"

"What can we learn by being curious about her . . . feeling in . . . learn from how she's holding her body, sense what she's feeling . . . what is there?"
"She's getting ready to come out . . . and she feels some tension . . . her forehead has a furrow."

"Worried?
"Uh huh."

"Can she reveal what the source of the worry might be . . . what experience in utero that has her worried?"
"I think my mom seems very sad. . . . She (the baby) needs to be held. . . . She wants to be here."

"But something about her experience with mother in the womb . . . mother's sadness sending a different message . . . see what else made her wonder."
"Her mother's in panic . . . she can't take a deep breath . . . she's tense . . . [mother or baby?] *The baby . . . I need to breathe now."* [Takes long breath.]

"Experiencing unusual physiology . . . flight or fight . . . tense . . . a shock to her system . . . so different . . . see if you can see how it affected her heart . . . this panic."
"Made me dizzy almost. . . . Made me think of being afraid of the dark."

"You needed someone."

"I had my sister and my Snoopy."

"But in your mother's womb, you had to deal with it by your-self . . . be curious . . . what you can learn."

"She wants someone to protect her . . . that's why in utero, I saw her curled up."

"An instinctive response to withdraw when something is dangerous . . . like being in a cocoon . . . holding this trauma to the heart . . . shocking . . . scary . . . what else . . . this is really extrapolating . . . if she sees through this lens what she has to experience, what does she come up with? . . . going to be brave?"

"Yes, she has courage . . . really sweet . . . she knows she's okay."

[Conversation about two-and-a half-year-old sister who wanted her to come, to be born.]

"Did her mother want her to come?"

"Maybe . . . overwhelmed."

"You, the adult with so much wisdom and love, make yourself known to this young child, this baby."

"Holding her . . . she needs to be loved more . . . precious baby . . . I just had a flash of her at age five, saying 'I'm here' . . . I wasn't going to give up . . . sweet baby though."

"Let her absorb this compassion, this holding you are providing . . . let her absorb all these energies into all of her being . . . this huge amount of love . . . let's see if she can show you how she's shown up in your life in ways you don't know."

"First thing that came to mind was ear infections . . . up until high school . . . terrible pain."

"What was mother's response?"

"*Sweet but stressed . . .her being there.*"

"When you weren't in pain?"

"*She did the routine, like a chore. She liked to bake . . . she liked to take us to sports in school . . . not like snuggling in her lap . . . I had my dad.*"

"An emptiness you've been aware of your whole life."

"*I had my sister. . . . I had my dad.*"

"But you started out with a relationship with your mother, and she wasn't always there . . . and that affected the unborn baby's heart."

"*That furrowed brow just came back.*"

"In your imagination as you are holding this baby, put your finger onto that furrowed brow, on her forehead, and with that touch let her know that you know that there is a gap that is bewildering, sometimes scary, but you, the wise compassionate adult, know and see this."

[She touched the furrowed brow.] "*She has a peaceful face. All lit up, soft . . . trusting . . . she feels home . . . she knows.*"

"As much as she can absorb the message that she's never alone . . . even in darkness, she's never alone . . . she's has a grownup adult . . . whenever you feel triggered, you can ask whether this is the unborn . . . you can say, 'I'm older, and I can send love, you're never alone.'"

Commentary

In the session it's apparent that the respondent, reporting from her child-self, avoided the pain of knowing that her mother neglected her. Twice by pointing to her sister, her stuffed animal, and her father, she said she received what she needed. I encouraged her to face how her mother's emotional absence affected the baby-self.

Though the respondent was holding the baby, I didn't see sufficient connection between them. There was no visible change in the baby. The baby's furrowed brow returning was an important clue. Once the adult touched the furrowed brow, transformation in the baby occurred, not before.

In working with babies, it's important to remember that touch is an important way to communicate nonverbally. Besides holding a baby, touching a baby's cheek tenderly or lightly around the lips communicates attention and caring.

I received a text message from this participant the next day, telling me, "I loved the experience. My daughter (who is fifteen) is ready to have a session tomorrow."

The Dance between Compassion and Empathy

In this Child-Heart session, the respondent is a highly intelligent, very conscientious spiritual counselor who has had many excellent teachers and exposure to a variety of healing modalities. She's married and has a MBA in marketing. Despite her achievements, she has current issues and volunteered to be a "test subject" with the Child-Heart method. I've guided her in several sessions. She's used it on her own and with her own clients as well.

In the following session, she describes her current challenges with fear and anxiety.

"Fear that has no logic to it—if I have numbness in my hand . . . or my hearts beats fast, I think there's something wrong with me . . . I have hypervigilance . . . my body isn't safe . . . my body's going to kill me. That the theme."

Her other issue is feeling rejected by someone important to her.

"The newborn holds so much . . . you don't know through the ages [of childhood] you've been through how many experiences were made worse by the scarring you had . . . having to meet up with the child who is ready to release . . . don't know who it will be."

[We move into guidance to deep relaxation with emphasis on body, connection with Mother Earth, what is most sacred (Divine Mother), and stressing the sense of safety.]

> *"There is a sense of frantic, a shakiness, uncertain about life . . . a young child, don't know how old exactly . . . all over my body . . . I need to be a witness as the adult, witness the shakiness in the child."*

"You can't carry the shakiness in your adult—you need to be solid in body when you want to be a witness . . . use this as the signal of the child's presence . . . thanking her for showing up."

> *"I feel it in my solar plexus, in my front body, that gripping . . . to be an adult, I'll look and find the young one and . . . take some breaths, and I think the way to do it is activate my heart, my compassion; that's how I can get out of my young one into my adult . . . I am more grounded, and I'm looking to the young one who is just jumping up and down; she's in chaos—frantic; so uncomfortable in her a body. . . . She's a few years old . . . my conscious memory is that I was kinda happy . . . out in the wild, on the farm . . . what I see is that she's terrified."*

"Don't need to know what happened . . . looking with compassion."

> *"Once again I'm challenged because I feel in my solar plexus what she's feeling . . . once again I must ground . . .*

embody the Sacred energy as well . . . [long pause] . . . Okay, so the adult me is calm; the young one is just having a conniption-fit, and so I let her know that I see her and let her feel what she feels."

"Make your presence known."
"How do I do that?"

"Imagine you're standing in front; maybe hold her hand . . . in your imagination, imagine your compassion, and with your intention to connect . . . to let her know that you're here. . . . You want to be with her, and you want to see whatever she's going through . . . what is happening in her heart."

"This is good . . . [long pause] . . . she's calming down a bit, and she's just crying . . . she's saying she's so scared . . . she's so sacred."

"I sense that the crying is less frantic . . . perhaps getting close to the pain in [her] heart . . . important."

"She's just so forlorn and so hurt . . . she's crying; she's heaving . . . don't remember crying like that as a child . . . her pain is so deep; it just cuts right through her . . . it feels like more than she can handle."

"Yet she has; she's being so courageous to have this, and she attempts to live life . . . she gets overwhelmed . . . doing the best she can to survive . . . to protect herself . . . much to thank her for."

"She's kinda turned away . . . she's standing by my knees, just leaning on me . . . she's calming; I can feel her heart, a very tender heart . . . and she can have a tantrum again . . . a wavering feeling in her heart . . . yeah . . . it just feels like her heart was broken in so many pieces . . . there is a sense of wanting to grab the different pieces of the heart and bring it back . . . So my solar plexus is tightening

again . . . ground again . . . wonder whether there is any value in exploring the connection between what the child is feeling with what the adult feels . . . how do we do that? . . . The adult that feels 'am I safe, am I going to die?'"

"Let's see what young child will come forward."

"I see an older me . . . this one is the one that moved to . . . that immigrant child . . . I have met her before, guess she still needs attention . . . doesn't know whether she's going to make it. It's foreign land; she doesn't speak the language. Parents are fighting about money. She feels so unsafe in her environment, lived in skid-row for the first couple of years, drunks on the street . . . at her cousins' house, two deaths . . . a lot of turmoil . . . so this child's heart spans over a four-to-six-year period . . . how do you do that?"

"Doesn't matter; basically we deal with who shows up. You know the basic circumstances, general situation, no sense of safety."

"Mother was paralyzed, thought mother was going to die, and the two deaths . . . I don't know, I don't know."

"See if you can remember or see how this immigrant child . . . how she experienced her body."

"There's an image of me going to school, my first school. My mother sends me off by myself. She just waves me off . . . I am scared . . . eventually I found the school by myself, but I was so scared . . . walking through the project, low-income housing project. I had to go by myself . . . my mother had to work . . . I just see her waving me off, 'go by yourself, go' . . . and I was very scared."

"I don't know whether this is helpful, but as you describe your situation in that period it's as if every cell of your body is filled with fear . . . the trauma of not knowing the language, where you lived, what you could feel, hostile . . . no sense of family or mother for any support, so the amount of fear compounded with your history, see if you didn't absorb fear in every part of your body."

"Yeah, well, there was a lot of trauma, but it was normal. . . . This is what happens to the immigrant child. You know the prejudice. The menial jobs my parents took . . . the prejudice . . . fighting in the schoolyards . . . they found, there was blood . . . a lot of crap . . . so I'm just going to let her feel the trauma and the fear of all of that . . . so her jaws are shaking inside . . . [long pause] . . . and that's just the beginning . . . see again, I have to be careful to be a witness and not feel the child in my body."

"Please get information about what she's experiencing . . . she needs the strength, witness, and compassion of the adult . . . not collapsing into the child, it doesn't work."

"That's really my challenge . . . okay, I'm putting my heart online for her." [Long pause.]

"Just staying there in your body and in your heart, and witness . . . so much trauma and so much fear for so many years . . . entire life up to this point, actually."

"All through my childhood and some of the young adult."

"Here's the message: there is nothing else to absorb but fear . . . alarms about safety because there's nowhere to go . . . your body is the alarm system that is set permanently by all these years of being so scared and having nobody there . . . appreciating that

that's how it evolved for you . . . felt in the solar plexus but really it's in your whole body."

"And so it's like . . . to witness that child . . . to allow her to have safety . . . I'm in essence retraining the nervous system of the young one, have her feel safe . . . I will sit here with her through this and be the adult.

"So the important piece is my body alarm is preset to freak out when there's any sign of danger . . . so through the power of consciousness in witnessing her having those experiences and letting her experience safety, then I can rewire her nervous system to safety . . . there is hope.

"I would be curious, I will explore this myself when the alarm system goes off like that . . . I will continue on my own."

Commentary

It was clear that this respondent needed reminders to stay grounded and not be her usual empathetic self. (I use the word "empathy" here as the ability to feel what another is feeling.) The adult who feels what the child-self feels knows her feelings but always needs to be *a compassionate witness*. It's the strength, grounding, and compassion of the adult as a witness that enables the child to reveal her secrets.

What she said about her session: "I felt like I had retrieved a part of myself that I had abandoned in shutdown mode. So, it's like bringing me back to more and more wholeness as I contact that terrified child's heart."

When you approach a child-heart, the hidden pain may not be obvious to you. In order to connect with her heart, use your imagination and compassion to know as best you can what she's feeling. You don't use your mind to *analyze*, but you *imagine* what the effect of the trauma has on her heart.

∾

These transcripts illustrate how the process unfolds depending on the individual's circumstances.

I hope the shortened version of these sessions preserved the precious revealing of the child-selves kept safe in the participants' hearts. To me, they reveal the amazing connections occurring. Every Child-Heart session I've guided left me in awe, both during and after the session, of the power of what I felt privileged to witness.

I hope reading through these sessions results in your being eager to discover for yourself what it feels like to connect with a young child-self. You will find additional transcripts at my website.

~

JOURNALING QUESTIONS:

1. As you read these transcripts, what were your reactions to the material in them?
2. Did you identify with any aspects of the experiences described?
3. Do you have questions about the Child-Heart method? Please check my website and/or contact me with your questions.
4. Record any signs of the two-year-old that you are seeing in your everyday life.

EXERCISE:

1. Complete a Child-Heart session using an open invitation to the child-self who is most eager to connect with you.
2. Write in your journal what you learn from your child-self and how you felt after the session.

[5]

BELIEFS AS ACCESS POINTS TO THE CHILD-SELVES

Chapter Three focused on intense emotions that linger or are overreactions as a means to connect with a child-self. Other ways are through the beliefs, defenses, and strategies that form the layers of protection around the wounded heart. The reason we focus on these layers is because they are also access points for the inner children.

When you notice these layers, you realize how long you've had them. Because they form early, they are quite limiting. Yet they are the patterns that define your life, so awareness of them is very important. In this chapter, we will look primarily at beliefs.

The upsetting emotions discussed previously are not separate from beliefs. In fact, it's usually because we hold certain beliefs that we become upset. For example, if you have a belief that the world is not a friendly place, and you hear news of chaos and violence in the world, your early belief could be touched. Then you may experience a strong sense of distress and/or fear. If you have the belief that you are "unimportant or worthless," and someone criticizes you, you feel bad about yourself. That situation touches an early wound.

I've organized beliefs and strategies into two separate sections to distinguish two layers of the protection used by the young child. How beliefs and strategies express themselves in life is not as distinct because they are related—strategies come from beliefs. We'll discuss strategies in more detail in the next chapter.

How Beliefs Define Your Life

When you read the literature on beliefs in various wisdom paths, cognitive-behavioral psychology, and self-help/self-empowerment, you learn how beliefs are the source of your patterns and your view of yourself, the world, and your life. Beliefs come from our culture, family, peers, and early wounds.

For example, this concept is found in Don Miguel's *The Four Agreements* in the need to escape the "Dream of the Planet" (the beliefs that come with the conditioning and programming we receive) and the Buddhist's aim to move beyond *maya* or illusions (because we all suffer from our belief about what reality is).

All current psychological systems and strategies to transform our negative beliefs emphasize the power of beliefs to maintain or change patterns. In sports, coaches point out how the four-minute mile was believed to be unachievable. When Rodger Bannister broke that barrier in 1954 by running a mile in 3 minutes and 59.4 seconds, he changed the previous limiting belief for everyone. He was the first, and others followed him.

If you search for "power of belief" on the Internet, you will find many examples of how beliefs create your world. Empowerment coaches help you discover and change your long-held beliefs in order to change how you see yourself and the world around you. Dr. Bruce Lipton's *The Biology of Belief* provides evidence for how our thoughts, positive and negative—that is, our beliefs—affect the expression of our DNA.

Your beliefs provide the subtext for how you live your life and how you view yourself and the world. Don't take anyone's word for this. Take a moment to consider the influence of beliefs as I guide you through your day.

- The moment you open your eyes in the morning, what you do next, and what you see come through your beliefs. Did you have dreams? Do you believe them to be nothing but the random creations of your mind, or do you believe they provide messages for you?
- What do you consume? Coffee, first thing? Fast breakfast, no breakfast, a healthy first meal? All of your choices come from your beliefs about your need to be alert, what is healthy, and what you believe are your priorities.
- As you move on to your day: what are your beliefs about work or career? What do you believe about having to work, being the provider or not? What beliefs defined what your adult path is? Do you believe you should enjoy life and thrive or that you deserve no more than to survive?
- Do you have a family, immediate and/or extended? What are your beliefs about what a family is, what your role is, and what you believe you can expect?
- In other relationships and friendships: What are your responsibilities? What do you believe you should provide and deserve to receive?
- In relationship to the country and the world, do you believe that the nation you live in is the best place on earth? What do you believe are your responsibilities in the world?

How Beliefs Are Your Blinders

Your beliefs serve as templates through which you view and interpret the world. Do you know how racehorses are fitted with blinders so that what is happening on either side doesn't bother them? The blinders keep their focus straight ahead. Once you become aware of the beliefs that narrow your view, you might want to remove what blinds you.

More questions:

- What do you believe about who you are?
- What are your beliefs about life? (I remember a Jewish professor friend telling us what his mother said to him: "What? You expect life is about having fun?")
- What do you truly believe you can accomplish/achieve?

Optimism Versus Pessimism

One easy way of seeing how we filter what we see in our world is through the lens or beliefs of optimism or pessimism. Optimists see what is positive about a situation, and pessimists see the negative side.

An example of optimism is "seeing the glass half full." I spoke with a young man who at twenty-nine has the diagnosis of multiple sclerosis (MS). How many of us would sink to our knees to hear that diagnosis for our future? Instead, Lucas declares that MS was the best thing that's happened to him. It clarified for him what was important to do in his life, and what or who to invest in. Before MS, he was confused; now he's clear.

Like any set of lenses, there are advantages and disadvantages to each. Optimists may disregard danger signs and not get the whole picture. Pessimists tend to see only confirmation of their dark views and never see opportunities to change or celebrate.

The Origin of Beliefs

Specifically at the time of wounding, even before the young child had language, she "decided" on a view of herself, the world, and life. If she was abandoned or abused, to "make sense" of her experience, she concluded that she wasn't *worthy, good enough, important, lovable,* or *deserving* of any good.

Feeling alone after the shock of being wounded by not having her needs met, she decided that *the world is unfriendly/ dangerous,* and it was *reasonable to be always fearful.* Feeling abandoned and believing that there was *no one to help her*, she may have concluded that she only had *herself to rely on*, thus believing she must be *independent and self-reliant*.

Here is a list of possible beliefs formed early in childhood. Take your time in viewing the list. Pause at each one and review the experiences in your life that verify whether you hold any of these beliefs.

- I am alone.
- I have no control; I need control.
- I'm not important, worthy, deserving of attention, lovable, enough.
- Having emotions is weak and wrong.
- I'm in danger. I am not safe.
- I am right.
- I can't stand it.
- I am special.
- Making mistakes is wrong.
- Anger is bad
- I am at fault most of the time.
- I am never to blame for anything going wrong.
- I am entitled to whatever I want and need.
- No one cares about me.
- I have no right to exist.
- I have to take whatever life hands me.
- I can't trust anyone.
- I can't get the love I want.
- I don't belong.
- I'm valued if I'm useful.
- I'm misunderstood.

To illustrate another expression of a belief, let's look at Dan, a young musician who complained of constant anxiety. Abandoned as a baby, he cannot talk himself out of the belief that he can't trust anyone. "I have issues with trust," he told me. "I look often at any sign coming from my girlfriend or mother to see whether I can trust them."

Beliefs that Come from Others

There is another important source of belief. Beliefs about self, life, and the world can also come from others. For example, while harshly spanking or beating a child, the perpetrator might say things like, "You are wicked/stupid/worthless." Or "You deserve much worse," "You always do mean and horrible things" or "You don't deserve to be alive."

Impoverished parents may instill the beliefs that "Everyone else gets ahead, but not us," "If you work really hard you'll get ahead," "No matter what you do, you won't amount to much," or "Quit dreaming."

Fearful parents might voice beliefs such as "This is a world in which people like us don't get a break," "You can't trust anyone; they are all out to get you," "You can't be happy for long 'cuz something will trip you up," or "You can't be too careful because something is waiting to get you."

I have an unusual story about the source of beliefs. I learned that I carried beliefs from my ancestral lineage, which I described briefly in Chapter 1.

Always wanting to learn more, I had an adventure that continued the thread about my ancestors. In my exploration of alternative healings, I learned about *ayahuasca* as used by shamans to enter mystical realms. Like many others, I wanted mystic visions and experiences. LSD never seemed like an alternative for me, and the shamanic guidance for *ayahuasca* intrigued me.

A dear friend and I prepared ourselves for the ceremony by dietary detoxing for two weeks before it. As part of the ceremony, the shaman asked us to set our intention for the ceremony. Strangely, I said "purification." I've wondered since why I said that.

Yes, I had beautiful images at first, but they were brief. Instead, a long night of purging followed—physical, emotional, and spiritual. After others had transitioned to more usual experiences, I was horrified to realize that I was still stuck in that space.

It was "hell"—absolutely no escape, no rescue, giving up repeatedly, pleading for an end, resignation, acceptance. At first I cried out in agony; I purged again and again. I danced crazily between willingness and surrender and grasping for control. The experience persisted quietly but continually until, in the early hours of the morning, I was out of it.

During the ceremony I had received a message from the shaman that it was time to let go of the pain and burden of my lineage. In the near-trance state of *ayahuasca,* I had no idea what he meant. In the morning debriefing he acknowledged my warrior passage and purification. Mostly I felt much relief—I had made it through hell. I was at peace and joyful.

I look at this experience as my dissolving the beliefs of being powerless, less than men, deserving no independence and freedom; how being female I believed I had no voice and nothing of value to express. I would not choose to cleanse my heart that way again. I'm pleased to know about gentler paths, and I created the Child-Heart method with this intention in mind.

Should, Always, and Never

If you watch your thoughts and what you and others say, you will find automatic use of the words *should, always, never.* To illustrate how ubiquitous these are, try to stop yourself from using them. It's not easy.

When we use *should,* we are expressing our beliefs about how to live. For example, many of us think that we "should always obey the law," or you tell yourself, "I should always show up on time," or "I should never be violent."

The words *never* and *always* point to exaggeration—suggesting strong beliefs behind the words. "I've never had anyone care about me." "I've never done anything right." "I always make mistakes."

These words are excellent indication of the voice of the Critic or Judge. Perhaps noticing the use of such words would lead you to your belief in perfectionism, or the belief that you need to be right. Regardless what it is, these words help point to ways of finding child-selves who invested in these beliefs.

Awareness of Beliefs and Choice to Change

Have you had the experience of looking at new cars and finding your favorite on the road everywhere? The time spent concentrating on such a project creates a change in perspective. That model now stands out from all other cars wherever you look— this is called the "Baader-Meinhof Phenomenon."

Awareness of beliefs works in the same way. Once you've identified a belief, you see how it operates in more areas of your life. Once you become aware of beliefs underlying your choices, you become aware of more beliefs, and these frequently point to the two-year-old.

Next muse on the consequences of having each belief. Do you want to change limiting beliefs to those that free your potential?

It's important to identify your beliefs so you can see how more aspects of your two-year-old operate in your present life. The Child-Heart method also uses beliefs to access child-parts. An invitation can be worded like this: "Will a child-part that knows the source of this belief about 'being bad' please make herself known?"

When you bring a compassionate witness to a child-self, the grip loosens on those intense reactions that fuel the belief. With each completed Child-Heart process you integrate another part of your young-self.

Child-Heart Processes Involving Beliefs

The following sessions don't all start with a belief as the access point to a young child-self. However, beliefs become part of the resolution for the process.

In the first transcript, Lilli sought a child-self related to what was currently troubling her. The session ended with her discovering a belief that a child-self held. In the second transcript as well, the respondent started out with a feeling of shame, but resolution came with the message, "You're okay," which I call an *antidote belief* to how he felt.

Belief: You Need to Hide Who You Are

The following session is the most recent that Lilli went through (described in Chapter Four). Recent events in her life troubled her. She was open to inviting whichever child-self could offer her the information she needed.

"Ten years old . . . been seeing her for several days, maybe twelve years old . . . sullen . . . serious."

"Make your presence known."

"She's acknowledged that she sees me. . . she looks like she's about to cry . . . going to ask her whether she can show me what is . . . she just doesn't feel loved . . . she has to be quiet, so she's hiding who she really is . . . she had a very serious side she couldn't show anybody . . . I think that people had a perception of me that I was a happy-go-lucky kind of child, nothing could bother me. My sister said that about me—the most distressing situations didn't seem to distress me. But it was hidden."

"Having to hide that aspect of you. How did that feel?"

"Feels like a big burden, very heavy burden [for a] very long time because I wasn't even aware of it."

"To be isolated, to be alone with this sense of having to hide . . . what was her reaction?"

"Devastating, but she's making me understand that she hid her brains, that she was actually a very intelligent child but it would have been too threatening, particularly to my mother . . . she had this obsession with my brother's IQ, how brilliant he was . . . no room in the family really to have brains."

"So out of compassion she hid her intelligence?"

"My sister never had to hide . . . she was artistic; Mother wasn't threatened because she was artistic, and it was valued . . . she couldn't deal with another bright child . . . a huge burden. The sense I'm getting is that I've been running from it my whole life."

"Her reaction, 'devastating,' feels like . . . sharp, dark energy . . . quite wounding."

"I think that little Lilli is very good at hiding . . . I had anorexia after my brother died . . . my father's cousin, a Jesuit who taught at the university . . . he took my sister under her wings, he was worried about her . . . he thought I was fine. When he found out . . . he was beyond shocked . . . because everyone assumed I was fine because I had this very cheery disposition. I had really learned by then; I was a master at hiding things. It must have begun with this little girl we are meeting today . . . looks to me that she's relieved that she's been able to tell me . . . feeling so much grief for her now."

"And she must feel tremendous loss . . . the life she could have . . . herself in fullness."

"What I did to deal with this, I got involved in oddball things . . . I went sideways . . . I couldn't take the place I really wanted to take."

"For this child, this ten-year-old . . . all the child-selves in between . . . she first mentioned that she didn't feel loved . . . like the anorexia was another way of showing that love hadn't touched her heart . . . we have compassion for that lack."

"I'm seeing that all was done . . . it wasn't deliberate . . . people caught up in their own agendas and not being able to see underneath the surface . . . I'm sure it goes on in every family, I've done it too."

"But right now . . . let's be present to this ten-year-old . . . when it's the right time . . . have her connect with the love she's always wanted . . . honoring and appreciating all her gifts and intelligence."

"She just wants to be held . . . saw that the small Lilli was very caring of her mother, always doing stuff for her, always trying to protect her."

"Sacrificing herself."

"I'm going to sit with this part . . . journal about it . . . think about what it means for my life now."

"So she's free to let out all that was hidden, giving it a chance to express that in the world."

"Yes. . . . Thank you . . . [this is] very powerful for me."

Commentary

Lilli has been through many Child-Heart sessions on her own and with my guidance. When enough time is spent with your child-selves, you can become aware of them in your everyday life, as Lilli described. She needed a little guidance to stay on target by focusing on the contents of her wounded heart.

Belief: "You're Okay"

The following session is with Paul, a retired professional who sought ways to deal with his issues using a variety of modalities. These involved healing practices and techniques focusing on emotions for which he received practitioner training. His interest was a somewhat conscious effort to understand his difficulties in life, including anxiety, depression, and an obsessive-compulsive trait.

We started with his sense of free-floating anger.

"I feel shame too . . . I get the image of . . . someone choking me . . . I don't have a clear idea of age . . . it's just that the feeling."

"Can you see what he's physically experienced, the expression on his face? Or have a sense of what is happening . . . emotional dimension . . . what comes to mind?"

"I don't know how much separation I have from the image. There is this real feeling of helplessness . . . unable to defend myself . . . now something's happening . . . I'm kinda lifted up in the air so really am helpless. . . . I'm being lifted . . . being choked."

"So stay with that young self . . . witness what is happening . . . [long pause] . . . What's the fear like? Any shock?"

"Yes, disbelief . . . I can't believe that this is happening . . . have no idea of who it is . . . I feel shame. I don't know whether because it was witnessed or I had done something wrong."

"Stay with the sense of shame ... if your body could reflect how you feel by taking a position, how would it express itself physically?"

"I would hide my face. The young boy says, 'Don't leave me. I would kill if I could.' There is hate too. ... Striking out ... hating. Making it personal to the person who is attacking ... I can hear myself ... I wish I were never alive ... don't leave me."

"We won't. Thank you for asking. What can we do for you?"

"He is asking to make him stop, and I still can't see any ... He's closing himself off; he's hardening his heart to this attacker. I can also hear him say no one can hurt me ... or not to show that he's hurt."

"Is there any sense of his air being cut off?"

"No, I'm not struggling ... Somehow I'm getting the sense that time is frozen in this scene ... action has stopped happening. Fine, can be with him ... I'm not still conscious ... It's almost like he's passed out or he's gone ... he's no longer in the scene."

"Will you call for him or look for him ... somehow he's found a way to escape, either by leaving his body or ..."

"I get a sense that the scene has changed, and now he's in the corner, quite small ... about five [years old] I'd guess. First, there's relief that he's safe now. Second, there is this feeling of really being alone ... doesn't know where to go ... there is no way to go ... he can't escape the overall situation. ... Momentary escape ... something like that could happen again, hurtful. ... Just hanging out with him."

"Does he see you? . . . Would you like him to see you? . . . So sit down in front of him, give him enough space, close enough for him to see you."

"There's a quality of his staring, he's staring into space . . . he's not focusing on anything . . . so I'm right there, unnoticed."

"Would it be okay to raise your hand in front of his eyes to catch his attention?"

"I did that; he recoiled like it shocked him or scared him. Letting you know that the feelings I'm feeling right now . . . think they are fear with a mixture of a broken heart. . . more than that, it's a broken spirit too. Somehow this is so . . . this event is that traumatic . . . things will never be the same."

"Prior to these thoughts, prior to his heart being broken, the events prior . . . any opening to see the pain that broke his heart; to see the pain that broke his spirit; the pain that made him not want to be here."

"A thought occurred to me . . . I don't know whether it's accurate. . . I don't know . . . an umbilical cord around my neck. . . never heard about it, about my birth process."

"Nonetheless, the truth of it, whether it's the exact details, you were threatened, possibly more than once . . . that your life circumstance were so cruel that it broke your heart . . . broke your spirit . . . it's that heart, the shock that we want to stay with."

"I'm staying with the feeling . . . there's no visual. . . . I see some kind of animal spirit that appeared . . . it's a baby anteater . . . what's a baby anteater doing here? . . . a smaller anteater . . . for some reason, this anteater is a distraction for the boy; he's struck by the cuteness of this animal. . . he's going about anteater business . . . somehow

the boy is finding some comfort in this, seeing . . . some-
thing about this animal . . . maybe there's something to live
for . . . it's not so bad . . . it's like a rescue, not an escape, a
rescue . . . it's like the anteater isn't everybody's favorite . . .
a kinship with me, we are misfits . . . somehow it makes
it okay."

"Follow the theme of being a misfit."

> *"Not angry any more, it's more defeated right now . . .*
> *that's the resolution somehow."*

"Giving up?"

> *"I'm not sure . . .maybe giving up on anger . . . I can't*
> *get the anger back."*

"Is there anything you're curious about it? Go back to the anteater . . . more to learn."

> *"I don't feel so alone."*

"Does the anteater have any message for you?"

> *"He just says, 'You're okay, kid.' . . . It really touches*
> *him. It's a message from an anteater . . . I don't know. The*
> *kid's saying, 'You're a better parent than my parents.'"*

"You're okay. . . . On an energetic level, can you see 'You're okay'
spreading from the ears to every cell on the young child's body?"

Commentary

The child-selves contacted in this session may not have been the
same; one was possibly younger than the five-year-old in the
corner. The child-self that was being choked probably dissociated
(left his body); dissociation will be discussed in the next chapter.

As a guide, I cannot hold to any expectation of how a session
will unfold. I stay present to what is before the adult.

When I brought up the free-floating anger Paul used to start the session, he couldn't feel it any more. He did receive a reassuring message that he needed to hear, although through a baby anteater. The message provided a positive note to end the session.

The Child-Heart Purpose

Once you're immersed in the discussion and description of beliefs, you may begin to detect them everywhere because they constitute the subtext of our lives. Some are advantageous, such as "See an opportunity to learn in every crisis," and some are limiting, such as "Having a handicap puts you at a disadvantage." (I wonder what Steven Hawking's beliefs are.)

For a Child-Heart session, you can start with a limiting belief that you have just as you can with an upsetting emotion. Since we operate with all aspects—emotions, beliefs, and strategies—finding a child-self means we may encounter all three, and possibly four if we include defenses. Putting labels and creating categories in these chapters represents an effort to clarify the different aspects involved in this process.

In some cases, whether something is a belief or a strategy is arguable. In the following chapter, we move on to describing strategies that also provide a subtext for your daily actions.

∼

JOURNALING QUESTIONS:
1. Study the list of beliefs and identify three you hold.
2. Describe how each manifests in your life.
3. Describe the advantages and disadvantages of each belief.
4. What do you believe about who you are? What life is? What your possibilities are?
5. Look around you and determine the beliefs that appear to underlie the life of people important to you.

EXERCISE:

1. Conduct a Child-Heart session using the most limiting belief you have.
2. Journal about what you've learned.

[6]

STRATEGIES BORN FROM WOUNDS

Two other ways to detect the presence of the two-year-old are through strategies and defenses. Strategies are more conscious and a little beyond reflexive responses when compared to defenses; they are less automatic and may be open to change. Strategies are the source of habitual patterns of our responses to people and situations.

In bypassing the mind and going directly to the heart, the Child-Heart method provides a unique approach to reprogramming these patterns. Therefore, discovering your strategies provides you opportunities to disable your automatic patterns and unlock your freedom.

What Are Your Strategies?
Strategies are important aspects of peoples' personalities. Below is a list of strategies to help you identify the ones you use.

- Naysaying
- People pleasing
- Giving too much, always doing for others
- Trying to control people and situations, often leading
- Avoiding intimacy or commitment
- Overachieving, super-conscientious
- Overusing humor, being the class clown, comic relief, jester
- Judging, criticizing

- Being overly independent and self-reliant
- Being a perfectionistic and being critical
- Manipulating and controlling
- Holding back
- Staying in your head (staying mental)
- Staying active and being a doer to avoid feeling
- Multitasking
- Grasping and being needy
- Being late, procrastinating
- Blaming, complaining, whining
- Escaping through addiction to food, alcohol, drugs, shopping, television
- Being overly responsible
- Being codependent
- Blaming yourself or making yourself the culprit to avoid attack
- Being glib or speaking in a loud voice

When you are able to see the strategies you or others around you use, you begin to see the lack of originality, aliveness, and spontaneity in the actions. It's like being automatons, robots—all because of strategies quickly adopted by a very young child. For example, in seeing someone arrive late to a special occasion, observers might say, "so predictable."

When you become aware that you are using the strategy of "trying to please everyone," for example, you might stop yourself and ask yourself, do I want to continue this way? Or if you notice that you're trying to manipulate someone's actions, you might give up your strategy and shift your stance, stopping your efforts to control. *Seeing such strategies may lead you to want to change to be freer.*

It's debatable whether awareness, having choice, and making a different decision is sufficient to permanently disrupt the automatic nature of strategies. Because these strategies and beliefs were formed early in life, they are programmed to create scripts for the rest of our lives. To complicate matters, some strategies are more deeply rooted than others.

You can experiment with trying to change a strategy you use, such as overachieving. Notice when you are in the overachieving mode and then make a decision to stop. See if you can follow through. One way is to use affirmations posted everywhere with words like, "You are okay. You don't need to overachieve," or "Overachieving causes too much stress. Relax." Learn for yourself how much effort it takes to change your strategies.

The Child-Heart method uses another approach. Diane, who we met in Chapter Three, had the strategy of being very organized and overly prepared in her life and work. After her Child-Heart sessions, she didn't feel she needed to work as much because she didn't need to prove herself any longer. Instead, she gave up the time set aside to prepare for an important event and had fun instead. She relaxed, and everything fell beautifully into place.

In other words, the Child-Heart method works toward resolving the wounds in the heart so that the adult can relax and trust more. She naturally releases strategies that came out of protection of the wounds. Rather than using will power or mind-based techniques (like affirmations) that use words to create change, change comes at the level of the heart where such strategies were first created.

How Upsetting Emotions Relate to Beliefs and Strategies

As I mentioned in the last chapter, I've separated beliefs and strategies into two separate sections to distinguish two layers of the protection used by the young child. How beliefs and strategies express themselves in life is not as distinct because they are related—strategies come from beliefs. For example, the belief that I am not good enough can lead to the strategy of always being good. When the strategy of being good fails, for example, when I do something wrong, I feel bad which touches on the belief of "not good enough." This is how emotions are related to beliefs and strategies.

May described how she felt safe and secure when her perfectionism worked. But her perfectionism strategy is demanding, exhausting, and stressful. She sometimes fails to be "perfect," and then she feels anxious and bad about herself. In short, when strategies backfire, they don't afford the full protection and safety for which they were intended.

Sources of Hidden Strategies

The two-year-old's wounds reveal themselves in many ways. The list above is by no means exhaustive, but my hope is that you will find the discussion of strategies provides a new way of looking at yourself. Besides spending time with these strategies to determine which you use, spending time with child-selves using the Child-Heart method can reveal how a particular wounding gave rise to certain strategies.

Judgments

I believe that *judgments* are a universal, unconscious strategy that we use to deal with what is troublesome in our world. Some judgments come from the programming we received in growing up: We absorb our family or community's values and perspectives. In other cases, judgments camouflage our deep emotional responses and issues pointing to a wounded heart.

Do you notice that you make judgments all the time? "This is bad." "That is good." "That is worthless." "He's wrong." "That's stupid." Underlying each judgment is a system of values that divide the world between what you approve of and what you don't. Nothing escapes: drivers, books, religion, races, weather, a meal, a restaurant, a dress, a car, this person, that business.

When you judge someone to be wrong or bad, it's because your beliefs and strategies define wrong and bad. One person can appreciate the aliveness, intensity, and talent of a young performer whereas someone else can see only the mistakes in the performance, revealing the projected strategy of perfectionism or criticism.

Underlying your system of right and wrong is the persistent strategy to make sense of your chaotic world by categorizing into right versus wrong, fair versus unjust. All of your templates of polarity (love/hate, good/bad, white/black, vengeance/ forgiveness) help to organize your experiences to lessen the chaos of complexities.

When judgments inevitably lead you to see yourself as good/ right and others as bad/wrong, they may alleviate and/or cover to some degree the anger of the wounded heart. In short, the mind uses judgments to justify so the pain can be pushed aside.

Regardless of the nature of your judgments, you might see that they arise not only from a need to be right, but from a need to have certainty, and perhaps a need for safety that comes from a system of right and wrong. These needs suggest wounding that has left the child feeling unstable (need for certainty) and alone, abandoned, and feeling unsafe. Then it is possible that the inner child signals her presence through fear.

Consider your judgments from the view that they may reflect your wounded heart. All of the beliefs, strategies, and defenses you have as a result of being hurt when very young created a set of lens to view your reality. Your judgments, therefore, can provide clues to your two-year-old's pain.

Seeing the Lessons in Trauma

Those who choose the spiritual path often use the strategy of seeing the lesson in any event that is disturbing or traumatizing. For example, if you suddenly became ill, this strategy prompts you to reflect on the question, what is the lesson here? There is no doubt much to gain from this strategy, but it may also help move you away from feeling the pain, fear, and anger related to having the illness. When looking at the young wounds in that way of asking for the lesson, the strategy leaves the young-heart still holding the pain, anger, and fears in secret.

One Child-Heart workshop participant, "Susan," a competent health practitioner with a Buddhist background expressed this strategy in her session. Susan has been a friend for a long time. In the last year she was diagnosed with breast cancer, underwent chemotherapy and radiation treatments, and appears to have made a full recovery. As we approached the wounded heart, she talked about the lessons she learned from the trauma. Susan continued to deflect attempts to move closer to the wounded heart.

Need for Control

Who can stand amid chaos with equanimity? Either you struggle to gain control of the situation or decide you don't have control and withdraw. Can you find times in your life when you saw your need to have control? When major events happen in the world, or in your personal or work life, it's easy to feel overwhelmed. There is disruption in the usual ways of acting.

I believe that feeling overwhelmed is the result of having intense emotional reactions to what is happening to you. You probably need time to sort out and feel the emotions, to look at the details in an effort to understand and then consider your options and devise a strategy or response. In the course of looking at your situation, you may realize that underneath it all is your need for control or a fear of losing control. In fact, don't many of your patterns reflect this need to control?

My Own Story

I sat with my need for control recently, inquiring about what lay beneath it. At that time I was very aware of feeling a need for control as I looked at those I cared about making the "wrong" choices. I realized how helpless I was to control their choices. I also saw how in the work that I produce I am ultimately helpless about how my work appears. I kept asking the question: what's underneath this need to control?

First, I found anger about each situation; I also found frustration, disappointment, and helplessness. In my imagination, I screamed out this anger. I saw an image of a collapsed child who was totally giving up, not wanting to try any more. She was small, contracted, and indifferent. I witnessed, acknowledged, and accepted all of the experiences. Happily, my need to control hasn't made an obvious reappearance after that Child-Heart work.

~

It is not uncommon to find young wives holding to the strategy of trying to fix or change their spouses, or to find supervisors and managers who use different strategies to control the behaviors of their supervisees. Parents inevitably run into the issue of attempting to control their children to keep them out of trouble, and to make the "right" choices in their lives.

In this time when some governments seem dangerously out of control, it's easy to be overwhelmed. The extent of the pollution of Earth is so vast that feeling helpless and without control seems natural. Learning what strategy you employ to deal with what is overwhelming is helpful. Some may just vent; others may use the strategy of judgment to feel relief.

If you know you have control issues, please sit with the situations that seem confusing and chaotic in your life. Can you find the fear, frustration, or anger that arises in the face of chaos and unpredictability? The strategy of trying to control protects you from upsetting feelings, feelings that can lead to a child-heart.

Need for Approval

I think that many of us have a need for approval. Approval indicates to the two-year-old that she's good enough, perhaps even lovable, and this seems to assuage a basic wound. However, you may not know why you use this strategy of seeking approval. It's natural; it's how you operate in your world. A Child-Heart workshop participant in Chapter Three described how her life was defined by seeking approval. She remembered how her mother taught her that she needed to dress to please even though she had other preferences. The strategy came early.

The need for approval encompasses other strategies like giving, being good, perfectionism, people pleasing, overachieving, manipulating, and controlling.

The problem with living for approval is that you can compromise your values. You don't stand up for yourself and what you believe is true. In short, you walk away from yourself; you betray yourself.

Some may find they overspend resources in terms of time, money, gifts, and attention to win people over. This is where women in our society often find themselves.

In a Child-Heart session that focused on my client's need for approval, she found a four-year-old child-self alone. After learning about what was hard for this little one, I prompted my client to ask what she could do for her four-year-old child-self. The child's response was "Don't leave me." I asked my client, "How can you do that?" The child, not the adult, responded: "Every time you care about whether someone's going to approve of your work, you leave me."

During the week following, the client reported remembering what the child said, and she felt much calmer.

Telling Stories

How often do you find yourself telling *stories*—repeated recounting of events about the past? It's important to learn for yourself how identified you are with these stories. They often are about being a victim; thus they reveal beliefs about a dangerous world, people you can't trust, and being helpless. Or stories can be boastful about achievements and successes, suggesting a strong need to be important or worthy.

Whatever the nature of your stories, you might think about your investment in them. Is telling stories a strategy to avoid being present in any situation? You may fear being open to the unexpected, so you fill the time and space with what you know. At some level, you may welcome the distance or wall that stories create so no one can get close to you. You may enjoy entertaining others to display your worth to others. What is behind this kind of storytelling is worth facing to find out how you are protecting yourself.

In short, many forms of storytelling can be entertaining and valuable. But there is a kind of storytelling that points to strong ties with past wounds. There's a hook that keeps these stories cycling and reveals a perfect access point to discover what child-part may be hurt and unable to move on.

Survival

Well-known to spiritual practitioners is the name of Sri Ramana Maharshi. At age seventeen he decided to learn what or who he was besides a body. Unusual for most human beings, he had a death-like experience while holding his breath. In his transition to death, he realized his true Self—he wasn't just a body. He was a spirit. His realization was the beginning of his journey to become an enlightened and beloved teacher of tens of thousands.

Very few have the will to suppress and overcome the instinct for survival. Try as we might, the instinct forces us to breathe when we try to hold our breath. Fortunately, most of us don't have to test our will or instinct to survive. But I saw the strength of this instinct underlying a resistant stubborn child-self who refused to give ground. It's as though he believed that if released his strategy, he would not survive.

I wonder how many of our strategies are tied to this survival instinct. Perhaps some strategies held by the child-self come from her belief that some of her strategies are her way to survive.

When I recently witnessed that tenacious hold on a strategy in a session with Paul, I remembered to accept what he presented—resistance to letting go of a strategy the adult found in the child-self. I also expressed appreciation for the spirit that was doing its best to survive the trauma of experiencing how his mother acted as though he didn't have needs. The child-self wouldn't let go of his strategy (pretending he didn't need anything from anyone) because he appeared to believe that if he gave up his strategy he would not survive.

What is Your Reaction to Learning about Your Layers of Protection?

As you start detecting your strategies, please notice what your reactions are, whether negative or positive. If you are shame-based or have a poor sense of self or low self-esteem, you may respond by feeling bad about yourself in discovering your beliefs and strategies. If you feel embarrassed or ashamed, or possibly guilty, you may feel as if I've pointed out your mistakes or shortcomings. However, please remember that by noticing these upsetting reactions, you are already in Child-Heart territory and are finding the results of your early wounding.

And remember, we *all* have these layers of protection, however we might hide from them.

As you become familiar with all aspects of finding your inner children you may learn to welcome the thorns. For now, become determined to end your suffering and look forward to smelling the roses.

Remember, noticing where your two-year-old is showing up is the beginning of your relationship with your inner children.

A Child-Heart Process that Reveals a Strategy

Leanne was unsure that she could complete the Child-Heart process because she had a bad headache that had lasted for four days. She was in pain before, during, and after the process. Leanne is a successful professional who runs a high-end business, attracting clients from across the country who fly in for sessions. Even as a teenager she knew how to create her dreams and new businesses.

Leanne has had bad headaches off and on for years. She unsuccessfully sought and tried many remedies, none of which worked to permanently rid her of her headaches. The session started *without* a specific intention of contacting a child-self who had some secrets to reveal about the persistent headaches.

"Whatever child-self wants to come first, you are welcome . . . What is happening?"

"It's just blank."

[I reassure her and then give instructions about remembering photos from when she was younger and then screening them for one that stands out, or picking one at random.]

"I'm sitting in my gramma's, like a La-Z-Boy . . . I was probably eight or nine . . . I was claiming this chair . . . Not sure if I was smiling; my eyes were bright; it was sort of like a soft but powerful expression . . . I think I was smirking."

"Pleased with yourself . . . enjoy that . . . things are okay right now. . . . Imagine putting yourself [the adult] near that chair, and see if you can, in your imagination, get an interaction going so that she sees you."

"I started off on the floor, and now I'm on the seat with her. [when asked, "Does she like that?"] Yes."

"When she's comfortable, ask her whether she has some secrets. . . . Let's see if you can, in your imagination, look into her

heart from the view that you have permission from her higher self... so you can share, witness, know, and accept what is
there."

"It feels... the reason I picked that picture is that...
this picture reminds me of innocence... shortly after that
I started to put on make up, perm my hair... something
happened to my sense of self-worth... I think it was
shame... I feel like in that picture, I was like a princess...
I look like one, I felt like one, there was a spark... I had
been beaten down... when I look at that picture, I see
a normal little girl and everything that came after that;
oh my God, what happened to her... the secret feels like
this energy that I'm trying to return to in my own life...
of the purity, the fearlessness... anything is possible...
flexibility... plasticity... also like, my family life... I
enjoyed it, and after that it got funky. I felt happy and
normal... Maybe it was... an inner confidence... like
Wonder Woman power...then I got beaten down and
started to care a lot... disgusting shit around me... the
poverty around me... why is there so much hair spray in
my hair... ghetto... makeup was all wrong... in this
picture, I look like a normal little girl."

"There may be strong pieces that keep pulling you back... that's
why I asked you to look into her heart... innocence and mischief... also held really dark pieces... I promise to return you
to this positive side... bring your curiosity and presence to the
dark places, so she doesn't have to hold them."

"What I get is that when I hit up against something, it
took a lot of strategy to figure out how to get into the chair
like that... I think the heart is... if I could just be normal,
I could be lovable."

"The experience in the heart left you feeling unlovable . . . some things happened to make you conclude that you weren't unlovable . . . what happened?"

"I think not having consistency . . . a father that wasn't around. I knew very early on that something was wrong . . . [I was] about four. I remember that my mom left me with some random person . . . who just had a baby and . . . just left me with the baby. Basically felt that she had left me for a lifetime. I couldn't figure out how to make the baby not cry . . . the police and social service people came."

"Let's be with this four-year-old . . . imagine how this affected her heart . . . so much inconsistency already. . . . might feel afraid."

"Felt afraid and like 'How do I figure it out?' . . . overwhelmed . . . okay like you got to build a rocket ship; but how do I do that; I don't know how to do that . . . I think it connects to what is happening in my life right now . . . feeling as I'm growing that life is pushing me in a new way, direction . . . oh my God, how am I going to figure it out? . . . not knowing how to let it unfold . . . it's hypervigilance and overresponsibility."

"Exactly . . . because in that experience you were alone; there was no one there. You had to figure it out . . . all these strategies of using your intellect and resources you had to figure it out because you can't depend on anybody . . . the way you are going to survive and thrive in this world, it's all on you . . . no back up . . . it's scary and overwhelming, but you have this spirit so you won't give up, you didn't dare . . . so I want you to capture what's in this four-year-old's heart, which is . . .being left."

"It just such a core pattern . . . I feel it in every single experience."

"So now take ... the adult who knows the continuity of this pattern and all the elements, be the adult who trusts the universe, ... just be present ... bring this adult ... to this four- or five-year-old heart ... say something like, 'I want you to know that I am here; you are not alone' ... see if you can make a connection with her heart ... [long pause] see if she can take it in."

"She can take it in ..." [Long pause.]

"You might hold her in a way that would make her feel secure ... safe ... see if you can see her relaxing and taking it in ... [long pause] ... How are your hearts doing?"

"Good" [Long pause]

"You can stay there as long as you want to ... you can say 'I'll be back,' or 'When I feel some of your heart in my current life ... I can ask—Is this you?' so you can both feel not alone."

Commentary

The next morning I received a message from Leanne. "Thank you for an amazing Child-Heart session. It was wonderful ... I woke up with no headache. ... I am *so* happy."

The session revealed the possible source of Leanne's headache in the strategy she adopted early in her life: take on almost impossible tasks in order to feel good about herself. The defense of somatization (her headaches) is discussed in the next chapter.

The Child-Heart session also revealed the strategy involved in the kind of situations that are very stressful for her. The strategy came from her belief that she was alone, and some version of the belief that she wasn't "good enough." On the La-Z-Boy chair she felt like a princess, but later lost that sense of deserving and worth.

By providing the child-self a sense of comfort with her presence, Leanne's connection with this inner child gave her a corrective experience. This young-self (or other child-selves) probably has memories and secrets that resulted in Leanne losing her sense of worth, in her strategy to depend on only herself and her resourcefulness, and in who knows what else. Only more sessions with more child-selves will reveal them.

Are You Ready for a Subtle but Radical Change?

It you haven't examined these aspects of your personality, you are shortchanging yourself. Remember, "The unexamined life is not worth living," a statement that is attributed to Socrates. From an Eastern source, Lao-tzu, founder of Taoism and author of the *Tao Te Ching*, comes "If you do not change direction, you may end up where you are heading."

To decide to examine your life and to change direction can be scary. Change affects people that way. You lose your usual orientation or balance. You move into the unknown.

However, your other choice is to have your future merely repeat your past. When you take the time for self-inquiry to look at your life and yourself, you can gain clarity that you don't have enough of what you truly want. This perspective can give you courage to change. The Child-Heart method guides you to create change at a deep level.

The purpose of this long discussion about the strategies created to survive traumas is to bring awareness to the patterns in life that keep us where we are. Often this means being stuck and frustrated. I've emphasized how many of these elements point to the young child's conditioning and influences. When you realize how many of the layers of protection around the wounded heart occur at a preverbal, precognitive, or subconscious level, you may want to revisit them.

The language of the mind is not as effective for making changes where you want them. Those who work with hypnotic and visualization techniques are aware of the need to bypass the conscious mind and tap into the subconscious. The Child-Heart method also is a bypass of the conscious mind.

The language of the heart is stronger and able to affect the heart and its layers of protection. The foundation of the Child-Heart method is heart meeting heart. It provides access to the young Child-Heart so its burdens can lift off the adult heart.

When you move toward the undefended heart, you move toward what you want for yourself: peace, love, joy, and wisdom.

∾

JOURNALING QUESTIONS
1. Study the list of strategies and find three that you commonly use.
2. Discuss the advantages and disadvantages to each of these strategies.
3. Observe the strategies of people around you and guess at what strategies they are using. How do you react to your observations?
4. Do you like change? How do you respond to change? What underlies your answers—what are the emotions, and/or what are your needs?

EXERCISE:
Choose the one strategy you use that is most prevalent or the most limiting, and invite a child-self to connect with you using the Child-Heart method.

[7]

HOW THE YOUNG SELF DEFENDS

As we've discussed, layers of protection around the defended heart include strategies and defenses. These operate in an automatic way unless we make an effort to become aware of them. Otherwise they operate without interruption. Since they too come from early childhood, the wisdom of keeping them in place is something worth contemplating. This chapter will focus on defenses that are more difficult to detect than strategies.

Defenses arise whenever "attack" (threat/deprivation/trauma) occur, whether physical, emotional, or energetic. Some may meet attack with attack, but it's still in defense of the self. Others may meet attack by some form of defense such as caving, withdrawing, or going numb.

Defenses

When a vulnerable young child is hurt deeply, *defenses* in the form of automatic responses to the wounding (of abandonment, betrayal, disappointment, humiliation, and confusion) arise. They are reflexive actions taken immediately.

The commonly recognized defenses include:

- denial,
- dissociation,
- projection,

- rationalization,
- reaction formation,
- displacement,
- intellectualization,
- repression and suppression,
- sublimation,
- acting out, and a few others.

The purpose for learning about your inner children's possible defense mechanisms is to help you learn how the child-heart is protecting the wounded heart. Only those that are easily observed will be discussed in this chapter. Some operate so unconsciously that they are virtually impossible to detect.

Freud described defense mechanisms as the means adopted to avoid emotions and thoughts that the conscious person judges are too difficult to cope with. In the context of child-selves, these defenses help keep the responses to trauma hidden as secrets in the child-heart. As you learn about them you will see how these protective defenses remove you from participating in the present. When you operate out of the past patterns you don't see any situation from a fresh point of view.

The descriptions below, based on a list found at PsychCentral (http://psychcentral.com). *My* descriptions may not be clinically precise, but they provide a general sense of defenses for the purpose of seeing ways a young child defends herself.

Denial

Denial may be a less conscious response that serves to help people maintain their reality. For example, it can preserve your picture of a person or situation by refusing to acknowledge details you don't wish to see. These details disappear from memory because they are incompatible with your ideal picture.

People in denial fail to absorb the importance of crucial details. For example, a man or woman looking for a relationship might see a potential partner act selfishly or cruelly in relationship to someone else. In order to continue the relationship, the man or woman in denial will ignore these aspects of the prospective partner, and the significance of them disappears from awareness.

Another example is when people get into enormous credit card debt. Lost in the world of acquiring and spending, they deny the reality of having to pay off accumulating debt. They fool themselves into thinking that they can juggle their bill paying, hoping that money will magically show up. Denial helps keep them from facing reality until they no longer have a choice. Even then they may fight to keep their illusions going.

Denying something is an effort to preserve the perfect picture. We catch ourselves using denial only in retrospect.

Suppression and Repression

These are defense mechanisms used to deal with unwanted, undesirable feelings, or things you want to forget. Suppression is a conscious act of pretending the negative doesn't exist. Rather than expressing your feelings of being upset, you choose to be polite and diplomatic instead. Suppression is used as a way to stay invisible and thus out of the line of fire. For example, if I show how I feel, I may be punished or ridiculed, or the information disclosed may be used against me later.

Repression moves negative thoughts and feelings into the subconscious because they are unacceptable. If you came from a family where no one expressed anger, or where there was too much anger, you may repress that destructive "ugly" anger. Repression works as an unconscious damper to quiet disturbing feelings. An example is when a child whose parents view him as an angel does not allow himself to have any negative feelings that contradict their picture of him.

Repression is probably the defense that child-selves use when they hide the effects of trauma in their hearts. The adult therefore has no conscious awareness of them, no access to these feelings, beliefs, or strategies except through a relationship with the young child who trusts you enough to share them.

Intellectualization

It's easy for some of us to be mental, to move into our heads and away from our hurting hearts. We create a reason for what is happening and analyze the situation completely, whether it's something we or someone else did; the actual reasons don't really matter. Moving into the mind to avoid the heart is automatic for many, especially those who prize the intellect.

For example, a child reasons that his parents may be "excused" for neglecting him because they had too many children and could provide only so much. The movement away from feeling hurt or angry happens through rationalization.

Shutting Down or Becoming Numb/Silent

Shutting down is my term for becoming emotionally protected and invulnerable—it's as if you withdraw your ability to feel. Shutting down helps buffer a person emotionally from what is challenging or disturbing in a situation. Some may consider shutting down a type of stoicism, the building of a wall between the emotions and what has evoked the difficult feelings.

The defense of shutting down runs in my family. In the past I found myself shutting down in response to being angry. It happened automatically to remove myself from the situation even if relocation was not physically possible. I felt as if I was in a compacted safe-cell or cage. For others, shutting down means physically leaving to retreat into some chosen "cave," such as going for a long walk, having a long smoke, or having many drinks.

In a recent Child-Heart session, an adult male learned that he had created a stoic shield just before his first spanking. The child-self thought, "I'm never going to let them know how I feel, never let them have the satisfaction of seeing me cry or hurting."

Neither the child-self nor the adult appeared able to access the suppressed feelings.

Attacking/Striking Back/Acting Out

A natural response to being attacked or misperceiving that you are being attacked is to act similarly by returning blow for blow, physical or verbal. These actions are probably instinctive. They are definitely not a fully considered action.

We see many examples of this in bar scenes or in sports arenas. Men act out their frustration and stress. In marriages, one spouse has an affair and the other acts out by having one too. Driving fast and recklessly is a response to being angry—acting out anger.

Dissociation

Splitting off memory or awareness, an unconscious response to trauma, is called *dissociation*. The extreme case of dissociation occurs in what was once called multiple personality disorder or split personalities. In response to a traumatic event such as being tortured or witnessing violence, a child leaves her body. Then in her conscious memory, both the child-part and the event disappear. With full dissociative disorders, a separate personality or alternate personality is created and holds a set of memories. The current diagnosis in that case is *dissociative identity disorder*.

Dissociation regularly occurs with post-traumatic stress disorder (PTSD). The literature on the causes and treatments is vast. Cases of dissociative identity disorder and PTSD are beyond the scope of this book. What is important with dissociation and Child-Heart work is that child-parts chose to split off painful memories. In one case, the respondent couldn't feel a connection with his Child-Heart. "He's gone," was the report. The child-self was there "physically" but not there in his heart.

In a sense, all child-selves with their secrets have "dissociated" their intense feelings from trauma by hiding them in their hearts. What is different about the dissociation in the Child-Heart exploration is that with a dissociated part, there is nothing to connect with. Dissociated parts are a particular challenge in Child-Heart work, which I discuss below.

The Child-Heart method, however, uses the *model* of dissociative disorders in the description of split-off child-selves who hold a particular set of memories and responses to a trauma.

The method of Child-Heart helps young child-selves reveal the hidden memories and disclose the dissociated experiences. Although recovery of memories is not the purpose of the Child-Heart process, memories that were not conscious have appeared while using it. Besides the particular set of memories related to one traumatic event, other early memories return. Once the adult has made a connection with one or two child-hearts, the grip on dissociated experiences loosens.

Somaticizing

Some individuals handle their stress, emotions, and conflicts by expressing as physical symptoms whatever troubles them emotionally. The mind-body literature and practices informing alternative health programs address somaticizing, whether explicitly or implicitly.

For example, a migraine headache may result from having said yes to a request when you really wanted to say no. Or digestive problems result because you cannot handle the conflicts in your life, such as being angry about your job. You show up anyway while hating every minute there. Stress is probably the first sign in the process of somaticizing. When stress intensifies and becomes chronic, somatization may result.

Projection

When you believe you see something outside that is really coming from you, you are unconsciously casting your inner reality to outer reality; this is called projection.

Projection is involved in what Carl Jung describes as the "shadow." Since we push a significant number of our own negative aspects out of consciousness, we hate/oppose/fight when they show up in others. For example, if you can't stand arrogance in others, it's likely you are unconscious of your sense of superiority or specialness. It's ugly and not who you are, you insist. If you hate bigots, it's because you are hiding from your secret biases and prejudices. If you are intolerant of weakness, it's because your own weaknesses lay well hidden.

According to Jung, our charge then is to discover and own what is in our "shadow" so our conflict with the world will lessen. In other words, the more individuals explore their depths for shadow pieces, the better able they are to subtract from their conflicts with the world.

Projections occur often in couples when one spouse accuses the other of something hidden out of the consciousness of the accusing spouse. For example, a husband may accuse his wife of always trying to control him when in fact, it's the husband who is a "control freak."

As I was revising one version of this book, I had a dear, brilliant psychologist friend give me feedback. He had many suggestions. I took the feedback personally; I was upset because he didn't meet my need for appreciation. In fact, I was so angry that I wanted to toss out the whole book after months of investment of both time and money. This is an example of projection.

I projected my own lack of appreciation of myself on to my friend. In the course of dealing with this incident, I found a child-part who didn't feel appreciated, felt rejected, and got so angry that she felt self-destructive.

(Later I was blessed to see that child-heart in my meditation and the broken heart that held the self-destructive energy. And for the first time, I embraced this child-self. What a homecoming.)

This is an example of how the Child-Heart works—embracing what feels bad at first can lead to palpable relief and joy. It is an example of the whole purpose of the Child-Heart method of returning to the undefended heart.

Why Discover Your Defenses?
None of these defenses are bad. In fact, many are useful and appreciated for the protection and guidance they provide. But it's important to discover those that are limiting to find child-hearts that need healing.

Remember that we want to identify all layers of protection around the wounded heart because they are formed very early in our emotional development, many before we had cognitive abilities. Since the resources for making decisions were limited, the beliefs, defenses, and strategies are woefully limiting and primitive. Yet they define our reality and how we operate in the world as adults.

Child-Heart Sessions Involving Defenses
The purpose of the Child-Heart method is to discover the child-hearts associated with these defenses. Witnessing by being present and being compassionate to what is in the heart helps to relieve the tenacious grip of these limiting protective layers of beliefs, strategies, and defenses.

Somatization: Anger, Confusion, and Emotional Pain Somaticized as Heart Pain
After Diane had three impressive Child-Heart sessions, she called to say she had awakened with heart pain. She'd had this symptom intermittently for about twelve years, and remembered the first time being close to when her mother died. There was no medical explanation for this symptom. Here is an edited version of her session.

"Diane has a secret place under the avocado tree; that's where she goes when she knows things she can't talk about. She likes to sit there because it feels safe, and it's very pretty; lots of different colors of brown, and the light comes through the leaves . . . she likes it there. She doesn't know what to do because her father says mean things to her mother and she doesn't know how to stop it, she wants it to stop . . . she feels sad and helpless and afraid."

"She wants to help, a generous spirit."

"She wants to make the mean words stop . . . she sees them like these things that fly through the air, and they hit, and they hurt her mother . . . no one will stop it . . . and so she wants to stop it . . . she's very little . . . maybe three because she has a baby brother now . . . and Daddy never talked to her like that when we lived with Gramma and Grandpa. He started saying mean things to her, they are dark, and they cut, and no one sees it except me . . . and I want to say, 'Stop that' . . . but I don't because I'm afraid of my father because he locks me up, and let me be poisoned and they took me away and mother said, 'You should never have left that poison out there where a child could get.' . . . He said, 'She's so stupid and she ate it,' but I didn't eat it; it was all around, and nobody told me that it was all around, on the ground and the floor . . . and he told me not to touch those bags . . . he told me that if I touched it I would die . . . I'm not stupid, I'm a smart girl . . . somehow the poison was everywhere and then I was sick and I fell over and everyone was screaming . . . it was terrible, they were yelling at me, and I did not do anything . . . and afterward, they never said they were worried. They stuck things in my throat, and it hurt, and then when we came home they said 'She was so bad because she ate the poison,' but how come they left out the poison?

They lied to me, it wasn't just in the bag, and my mother screamed at my father and said 'You should never have left the poison out there,' and he said, 'You are stupid, and if she wasn't such a stupid girl she wouldn't have put it in her mouth'. . . . I never did that, and then they treated my father like a hero because he took me to the hospital . . . it was very scary. They didn't even care, except they just yelled at me. But my mother yelled at my father, but he said that we were all just stupid . . . it was my fault, I couldn't see it. . . . I never would have touched it if I saw it."

"It wasn't your fault . . . and you didn't have any support, no one seeing . . . it's as it you weren't important . . . I'm so sorry . . . you could see the truth, and to see it denied."

"I remember it, and I pretended I didn't remember it, but I do. I wasn't supposed to feel anything . . . .I never understood why I wasn't supposed to feel things, I thought there was something wrong with me . . . when I said something happened and then they say it didn't, who am I? I am this weird thing that doesn't exist."

"So young, you were rejected . . . abandoned . . . lost in that . . . a part of you always hid your true nature . . . if you come out as you are, you're just wrong."

"Yes, you're just wrong . . . you're not one of us . . . you're just this weird thing . . .I could feel safe under the avocado tree, the nice place along the creek . . .no one is going to tell me that I was all wrong."

[I spoke with appreciation to the child-self about what she experienced, the dark energies encountered, her spirit, and how she could see the truth, and I assured her that she'd done the best she could do with the threat of annihilation to comply and conform. "A strategy that helped a bit but didn't really protect," were my words to her.]

"You're never safe . . . that was the nightmare . . . I never felt safe, really . . . I remember from that moment knowing only that my survival depended on what I didn't understand . . . didn't know what I was supposed to be careful of, I couldn't trust people's words, and I was on my own . . . I remember thinking, 'Why didn't you tell me that it was everywhere,' but he never said that . . . my uncle . . . got mad at my father, 'You should never have left it out,' he yelled at my father. My father said, 'Don't be stupid.' . . . I thought when he said that, he didn't really care that I wasn't safe, he didn't care. It made my heart break [crying] it made my heart break because if he didn't care, who cares."

"Truly sorry that this blow to your heart was more than it could take . . . want you to know that a broken heart can mend."

"It's been broken for a long time . . . maybe that's why sometimes things felt so hard . . . that I would have to struggle, that's the reason . . . whatever I am working to get never seemed to be what I wanted . . . always felt like I was on a raft."

"I don't know whether this is right, but I have a vision of the original pure heart that knew only light."

"I think I have things that remind me that it can exist . . . the future Buddha, she has the most beautiful face, Miroku . . . many days I chant the heart sutra . . . I've never given up . . . the dream of the whole heart . . . after that, I couldn't hold a pencil well, from that day I practiced drawing circles . . . I thought the day I could draw the perfect circle, my heart would be whole . . . she never gave up on having the whole heart. She's very bright . . . I can feel

her coming into me . . . she's been alone for so long . . . she
doesn't have to be . . . so this is what completion feels like."

Commentary

Diane reported feeling very free and different for a week. Then one morning following a weekend visiting with three old friends, she awakened with a milder heart pain. One friendship seemed viable to her while she was troubled about the interactions with her other two friends. A few weeks later Diane came in for a Child-Heart session when her heart pain returned. She talked about her troubling friendships with four different women. "I think it's time to deal with my mother," she reported.

In that Child-Heart session, her child-self talked about all the things she had done to protect her mother from her father's terrible anger. Diane's mother ran the household in a disorganized manner. Since her father didn't tolerate disorder, young Diane always cleaned and ordered the house. In other ways, Diane put her mother's needs before her own, just as she did in her friendship with women. Diane saw how consistently her strategy played out throughout her life—she made her needs unimportant in relationships with women. After this session, Diane reported being free from heart pain.

A Dissociated Child-Self

In two Child-Heart sessions, indications of possible dissociated child-selves appeared. Paul, who we met in Chapter Five, said that although he could see the five-year-old physically, there was no one there emotionally. May, a successful health professional, came to see me with challenges of perfectionism, seeking approval, and anxiety. In one session she described a "scared" child-self without connection to any memory. In both situations, I found that focusing on the dissociated parts wasn't productive.

In another recent session, Paul found a five-year-old who was distressed because he thought he had wet his bed. In connecting with the young-self, Paul discovered strategies and beliefs he had adopted, such as hiding who he was, what he had done, and what he felt. He also noticed the tension the five-year-old held in his whole body. The revelations resulted in greater ease with some current issues in Paul's life. It seems that connecting with other child-selves who had memories and secrets to share, the five-year-old was "ready" for a compassionate connection. The "dissociated" child-self was also five years old.

Summary:
The Child-Heart method builds on the concept that hearts are wounded during childhood when the original safety of the child is disrupted by an event, large or small. Layers of protection inevitably form around the heart to prevent further harm. These layers are beliefs, strategies, and defenses. Beliefs and strategies are more often found in Child-Heart sessions than defenses.

The purpose of the Child-Heart method is to connect with young hearts to provide an opportunity to reveal secrets in the presence of a compassionate adult-witness. Because a child-self splits off with each trauma, holding a set of memories and painful reactions, many have multiple child-selves to gather for wholeness.

Although the journey within may seem strange and mysterious at first, what unfolds is often precious and ultimately rewarding. Why? The undefended heart, free from the layers of protection, is the source of joy, peace, creativity, and wisdom.

∾

JOURNALING QUESTIONS
1. Study the list of defenses to determine which ones you use most often.
2. Describe the advantages and disadvantages of the defenses you use.

3. Observe people around you to determine the defenses they appear to use.

EXERCISE:

1. Use the defense to find a child-self. If you can't find one, select a pervasive strategy you have.
2. Conduct a Child-Heart session to invite a young-self who knows this strategy well.

[8]

FINAL THOUGHTS ON THE CHILD-HEART METHOD

When you follow the protocol of the Child-Heart method, you encounter and interact with a young-self. Your capacity to witness, be curious, and have compassion deepens the relationship. If you are committed to your child-selves and to fulfilling your potential, you return to gather your "lost children" until you are home in your *undefended heart*.

As may be evident throughout my writing, the Child-Heart process is not about understanding or getting it through your intellect, it's about an experience: about being present, making a commitment, and creating a compassionate connection with your child-self's heart. *Listen to the Cries of Your Heart* invites you to spend time in self-inquiry and to use the Child-Heart method to heal your broken heart. *It requires practice. It requires time spent with yourself—meditating, journaling, and doing Child-Heart work.*

As you read through the chapters, you learned more about the nuances of the Child-Heart method. Although I started with a fairly simple method, individual differences became apparent. The more Child-Heart sessions I conducted with a variety of individuals, the more I discovered.

For example, there are individuals who complete a Child-Heart process in the first session. Within less than thirty minutes, a complete experience ends with a felt transformation in the child-self and/or the adult. A completed Child-Heart session, however, is not to be confused with completing the *transformation* that is possible using this method. Diane, for example, who has had seven Child-Heart sessions, more sessions than most, has experienced a most profound transformation.

Others, after their initial session, turn away from the method to resume their usual lives. These participants did not meet the *hearts* of the child-selves and therefore did not experience the full possibilities of this method.

I've wondered long about what may have happened for them. I concluded that it was clearly not the right time, nor the right method—or maybe they needed additional support and to learn to build trust in themselves, in life and in something beyond this apparent reality. Or perhaps the fear that seemed overwhelming to the child percolated up to the adult to stop further exploration.

Central Principles of the Child-Heart Method

In the sections below I discuss five central principles that are worth revisiting because they will help you to intuitively respond and flexibly adapt to certain challenges. There is clearly more to learn about child-hearts. Please let me know what you discover as you join us in this marvelous adventure.

Trust in the Power of Imaginal Space

As I have mentioned, the Child-Heart method has a strong foundation in its start in creating the place of imagination. When I guide people through this initial stage, I mention that when in deep relaxation, we enter the imaginal space where there is no time. The veil between the conscious and the less conscious is thin. All memory is available.

Many people have difficulty believing in the power of the imaginal space; it seems impossible. But it is necessary to accept the idea that "all things are possible" in this safe, sacred place for the Child-Heart method to work effectively. When I am in that imaginal space as a guide, it's magical.

The first surprise is that adults can actually encounter young child-selves and interact with them. The second is that with the adult's presence, witness, compassion, curiosity, and trust, a corrective healing experience unfolds. What I am suggesting to you may sound preposterous: that in the imagination it is possible to move back into the past and create a different experience for a child-self.

However, those who are familiar with trance work or hypnosis, past life regression, neurological repatterning, or any similar system know the power of relaxing the grip of everyday consciousness. In other words, deep relaxation brings an altered state of consciousness where there is both alertness and access to less-conscious material. Those who use visualization to help people make changes in their lives utilize this same space. You'll find many reports of successful people, especially athletes, who use visualization in their training.

One of the most famous individuals to discuss the use of imagination was Napoleon Hill, author of *Think and Grow Rich* (published in 1937, with more than 70 million copies sold by 2011). In a section of the book (which he hesitated to publish), this pioneer of personal development described a visualization technique. He created his "Invisible Counselors" that included wise men whose advice he would value.

After a few sessions, Hill found that the counselors gave him advice, information, and wisdom that he didn't consciously have. To Hill, they became more real than imaginary as time went on. Among the fifty advisors he invited were Lincoln, Edison, Carnegie, Emerson, Ford, and Paine—men Hill admired for certain traits they had.

Hill continued with his Council for months because he gained immensely from spending time with these great minds. In his book, he wrote,

I still regard my cabinet meetings as being purely imaginary, but . . . they have led me into glorious paths of adventure, [and] I have been miraculously guided past [scores] of difficulties . . . I now go to my imaginary counselors with every difficult problem which confronts me and my clients. The results are often astonishing.

I cannot provide proof that such travel in time can occur. Or that these interactions actually happen in "the past" for the child-selves and adults. I can only report what happened, and that they had significant effects on the adults—as if what happened in the imaginal space did occur. Adult Child-Heart participants report impressive changes that I've reported throughout these pages.

Remember to Ask Questions of the Child

Sometimes people struggle to build rapport with their child self. While others once they have a sense of rapport find it difficult to encourage the child to speak and reveal her heart. In moments when the session appears to have stalled in this way, the following questions are very helpful: "What can I do for you?" "What do you need?" Responses heard include, "Don't leave me," "Play with me," and "I need to know that things will turn out okay."

In a recent session with Dan, the young musician who had constant trust issues, I asked the young four-year-old self what he needed when he "appeared" to Dan everyday with doubts about trusting his girlfriend. The child-self said: "Acknowledge me. Don't ignore me." Hopefully Dan will remember to do this and his difficulty with trust will lessen.

Remember the unusual interaction that occurred with May, the health professional who felt anxious most of her days? In her Child-Heart session I was puzzled by how the adult could respond to the child's request not to leave. I was surprised when the child answered. "Every time you do something for approval or get nervous because of fear that you won't get someone's approval, you leave me."

Rather than making assumptions and more statements, I ask more questions of the child-selves. I am ready to be surprised by the wisdom that arises.

Amplify Compassion through Expressions of Appreciation

In some sessions, I created long monologues of appreciation directed to the child about what she had done to protect the growing child from further hurt. I expressed appreciation for the courage, resourcefulness, and the protective intent of the child. If strategies were clear, I also expressed appreciation for them. I could wax poetic about the possible effects of the trauma on the child, demonstrating my intent to see and understand the secrets of the heart.

One child-part validated the effectiveness of such expressions by saying that she liked it after I said, "I talk too much."

When you do this in your solo work, you build your capacity for compassion by expressing appreciation. You establish rapport and enhance the child's sense of safety. She has reason to trust through what you reveal—the caring and compassion in your heart.

Know When to Hold Your Child-Self (and When to Play)

Some Child-Heart participants spontaneously hold their child-self when they see the need. Although this is a natural response to make, I guide the adult to do more—to make sure to observe, fully sense, and interact with what is in the heart and *not stop* with just comforting. Contact with what the heart hides—bewilderment, feeling alone, terror, and pain—is crucial for a corrective experience for the child-self.

Especially in the case of a very young preverbal baby-self, the holding may be exactly what is needed to get the young-self's attention. In such situations, there is no other way to communicate compassion to the young being. The holding provides comfort and a sense of safety—what was needed at the time or what was taken away at the time to cause the trauma.

After the adult senses that the child-part is calm, she can assume that the child-part has felt benefit from being with the adult. From that point the relationship can deepen, so all "secrets" in the child-heart are out in the open and witnessed.

Once the adult presents herself to the child-self, the interaction between the two doesn't always follow a smooth script with a ready acceptance by the child. In one session I witnessed, the child stood shyly behind a wall, half in hiding. After she came into the open, she still wasn't ready for contact. The adult asked whether she could play with her. After the adult rolled the child's rolling pin and drew butterflies, the child-self warmed up to her.

It was after playing that communication between adult and child became possible. Eventually the child revealed her heart's secrets. For other child-selves as well, it became clear that the child-selves needed more time to feel comfortable and trusting of the adult to be ready for engagement.

In another Child-Heart session Dan, the successful young musician described above who complained about almost constant anxiety and a lack of trust of important women in his life, reported an unusual greeting from his child-self. When Dan made his presence known, the four-year-old young-self grabbed his legs. I guided the adult Dan to ask the child what he could do for him. The response was "He wants to play." The child ran around energetically as if playing Catch Me. The session ended with them in play, and then the following session moved into the work of the heart.

A similar response occurred in a first Child-Heart session with a client who had multiple problems, the worst of which was frequent anger. Craig made contact with a child-self who was waiting in his locked room for his father's return. His mother had promised a punishing spanking from his father, and he was terrified. When Craig made his presence known to his young self, his child-self welcomed Craig's company; he wanted to play.

In Craig's next session, the three different child-selves who came forward seemed more trusting of the adult, so deeper interactions were possible. In the latest session, a child-self revealed his fear of annihilation. Craig communicated with him to let him know that his fears were unfounded. The more time he spent with his child-self, the more Craig relished the role of being the parent he never had.

Accept "Completion" as Only One Step in the Child-Heart Process

I have been using the Child-Heart method for myself, mostly solo, for about nine months. It's becoming more difficult to see signs of my inner children. As I've written earlier, I am rarely triggered by anyone or anything. I laugh more often and easily. I see beauty everywhere. I feel light, not burdened with negative feelings or challenges. I am living my life purpose of bringing divine truth to individuals through the Child-Heart method. Recently I had a remarkable time with a partner in my spiritual group "being present and being still." I think I'm moving *toward* completion.

For a Child-Heart participant, one particular session can feel complete. After Diane's last session, when she remembered her father breaking her heart, she said, "So this is how completion feels." Afterward, however, she realized that there was more work to do. She felt a different kind of heart pain later. Evidently there were more child-selves to meet and bring home.

In an update between sessions five and seven, Diane reported that she used a modified Child-Heart process over several days. She spoke to her inner children and said everything she needed to hear as a child. Two very vivid dreams followed: the first was remembering her time before this present incarnation when she was a pure being of light. Many scenes followed that were her sudden and harsh earth experiences, which illustrated how the contrast of the light with the darkness in her early life shocked her.

Diane reports that she awoke the following days feeling happy—a magical transformation from terror and heart pain to happiness in less than six weeks. I call her my Child-Heart poster child.

In short: our hearts were not broken just once. Our young selves met trauma in different ways, and if we want to become whole, we need to gather all our lost children. They will keep showing up until there is no need to. When we have mended enough, we are in the undefended heart of our original innocence.

What Happens between Child-Heart Sessions

I wish I could be privy to what happens to Child-Heart participants between sessions, but I have information from a handful of individuals. As noted in the beginning of Chapter Two, once you learn about the Child-Heart material, you will notice signs of the child-selves in yourself and others. When you see them in yourself, the best you can do is acknowledge the child-self who is there. Remember the message from Dan's young-self: "Please acknowledge me." I found that when I acknowledge a child-self associated with an upset feeling, the feeling often disappears.

When regular clients report no change in the issue that we addressed in a Child-Heart session, that child-self usually appears again in the next session to more fully disclose her heart's content.

Diane reported that after her Child-Heart session about her mother, she spent time taking in the implications of the session for her and her relationships. What unfolded for Diane after the session led her to conclude that it was a "huge" session for her.

Child-Heart Participants' Ages

The general age range of clients and workshop participants using the Child-Heart is probably forty and above, with two exceptions.

Two teenagers, both fifteen, went through a Child-Heart session: one was a "volunteer," the other a client. They both reported that they benefitted from the experience. One called her session "very healing." The mother of the second teenager said that her son seemed lighter, as if a burden had dropped from his shoulders. He said he felt better, especially in his sports performance. A general ease settled in him, resulting in open affection expressed to his father.

Both teenagers are somewhat unusual in their maturity and their ability to be emotionally honest. In general, the younger an individual is who uses the Child-Heart method, the easier the work should be. There will be fewer years of living with early beliefs, strategies, and defenses that cement the layers of protection. Possibly more important for a positive outcome is the openness and willingness of any individual, regardless of age.

Note to Practitioners

Additional material for practitioners is available on my website. Included are more transcripts of sessions with commentaries. Practitioners and others who are curious about the details and nuances of a session can peruse them to learn more. I will continue to update them, especially when I encounter particularly interesting or unusual sessions.

Access to the practitioners' area with a Q & A section, and other resources will be provided after a consultation call with me.

Those who have a meditation practice and/or hypnosis training will probably ease into being a guide or doing solo work more readily than those who don't. However, recordings of the Child-Heart introduction to deep relaxation, for the creation of a safe place, and other Child-Heart guides to a complete process are available at my website to *learn* the techniques or procedures or to *play* for a session with a client.

A practitioner who is heart-centered and has practices to expand the heart's capacity to love, to be compassionate and trustworthy, will have an advantage. Appreciation of the sacred or the Divine Feminine and other spiritual capacities adds another resource for holding and help.

The Child-Heart method is only *one* way to do inner children work. Hopefully the experienced practitioner will use what is helpful and extend or deepen their inner child work by using material in this book. The best practitioners know who they are and how they work best—they will know what parts of the Child-Heart Method inspire and excite them.

To Women, Especially Asian-American Women

As I mentioned earlier, my cultural heritage is Japanese-American. I've revealed part of my challenges that came from the values I "inherited."

In looking back over the experiences connected with my Japanese heritage, I realize how a template of bondage existed in my beliefs and strategies. The patriarchal system in Japan and in the rest of the world has been in place for millennia. The lack of empowerment that women can discover in their child-heart is impressive in its depth.

This includes women of all ages.

It is my vision that women of all cultural backgrounds will unearth their freedom through this Child-Heart method or something similar. We cannot afford to waste our lives not living in our full expression; we deserve to be free from the burdens that weigh heavily on our hearts. Yes, the subject of another piece of writing.

Summary

As I mentioned earlier, doubts about the worth of my writing and the Child-Heart method arose from time to time. However, when I reviewed what happens in Child-Heart sessions and the changes in the individuals after fully meeting a particular child-self, I ceased to doubt. When I acknowledge the many synchronistic events that occurred in the last year related to *Listen to the Cries of Your Heart*, I believe that I am led and inspired to offer this gift to the world. The Child-Heart method is my current service to help individuals heal their broken hearts.

Remember, no one can escape from a wounding to the heart early in childhood. No parent in our society can provide constant, appropriate attention that doesn't have lapses, whether those lapses last a minute or days. The young baby or child experiences being safe and then suddenly feels completely alone in that time of lapse. Intense and difficult feelings judged to be overwhelming by the young child are hidden in the heart. Beliefs, strategies, and defenses arise to protect the heart from further harm.

People with defended hearts can be "successful" in the world, but all profit from moving toward their undefended hearts to experience the fullness of who they are. The undefended heart is the original heart of pure innocence, holding peace, wisdom, joy, and play. Who doesn't long to be peaceful and happy?

It takes courage and being in touch with your longing to "be all that you can be," to be able to listen to the cries of your heart. Commitment, patience, curiosity, and compassion are needed to gather your lost inner children to bring them home to your heart.

Listen to the Cries of Your Heart moves out into the world to touch the souls of individuals ready to bring wholeness to their hearts and balance to their lives.

Please let me know if you are one of these precious ones.

THANK YOU!

I imagine that you, a reader of *Listen to the Cries of Your Heart*, might be like me in some respects. I always wanted more from life and more from myself, but I didn't always consciously know it.

I never knew I was lost and trying to find my way out of confusion. From the Child-Heart perspective, early beliefs and strategies ran my life. I didn't know I was prisoner to those early decisions.

In the same way as many teachers appeared in my life to clarify my life purpose and path, I hope this book will help to provide a light to show you the way home to your heart and to what you always wanted.

I send blessings to you wherever you are.

My prayer is that the child-heart path to your inner children will help free you from the burdens created by early wounding and also bring you the gifts of the undefended heart.

Please let me know who you are, what your response is to this book, and contact me with any questions. You can reach me through any of the following:

- http://ListentotheCriesofyourHeart.com
- https://www.facebook.com/Child-Heart-244465205908662/

And of course, your honest review of *Listen to the Cries of Your Heart* is welcome to help spread the word.

ADDITIONAL RESOURCES

The following are available on my website:

1. Contact information: Anne@Childheartmethod.com.
2. Child-Heart sessions guided by me: fees for individual sessions as well as packages of sessions (discounted).
3. Six weekly classes and three weekly workshop sessions through conference calls or webinars to accompany the Child-Heart material. Schedule and fees found at http://Childheartmethod.com/classes.

   Besides covering essential aspects of the Child-Heart methods, these sessions will provide discussion of exercises and group guidance for Child-Heart sessions.

4. Transcripts of Child-Heart sessions: http://Childheartmethod.com/sessions.
5. Recordings for guidance: http://Childheartmethod.com/tapes.

There are recordings for:

- deep relaxation;
- for creating a safe place;
- for Child-Heart guidance to find a happy child;
- for Child-Heart guidance to connect with a child-self connected with an emotion;

- for Child-Heart guidance to connect with a child-self connected with a belief;
- for Child-Heart guidance to connect with a child-self connected with a strategy.

6. I use meditations by Miranda Macpherson, http://www.mirandamacpherson.com/in-the-sanctuary/; by Peggy Sealfon, http://www.stonewaterstudio.com/index.php?pr=Yoga_Nidra; and from Yoga Nidra meditation teachers on Youtube.

7. Sign up for my newsletter by visiting my website. You'll receive early notification of free gifts, recommended readings, new courses, and events, as well as new transcripts and suggestions for connecting with your own child-heart.

APPENDIX

Undefended Heart

Back then my six-year-old hands lock in prayer.
Penitent heart wills "Hail Mary"
to blend with acrid incense
make me holy.

Back then my tap shoes click on lit stage.
Hands kite around like a fledgling bird;
take a rehearsed bow;
wait for approving applause.

Older now
It's as if I was blindfolded
turned around
unblindfolded

into a new way of dancing.
I still hear my child eyes
plead to be enough,
but often now I find myself

in a limber place, no need for as many ovations,
overflowing ledger of merits.
My wrinkled hands lift undefended self
into a lifeboat boat, already saved.

I have become a wayfinder,
learning to navigate my ocean of life
one wave at a time and I wonder
what magical wind will blow through me

when *not enough* visits me again and I put up
a sand bar of defense?
But in this moment as I write this verse
my heart beats a deeper rhythm,

I hear giggles of my child voice
see tiny feet dancing just in the wiggle of it
humming tunes that erode me to my *enough* where
my breathing almost stops.

—Marianne Lyon

When I Was Seven Years Old

It was an ordinary Thursday afternoon. As Joey, a young boy, walked goofily through his neighborhood in Brooklyn, he whacked each streetlight pole he passed with a hefty piece of wood. He liked the reverberation in his arms, the kickback from that sharp contact. At about 4:10 pm, he whacked a light post. He whacked it good.

Suddenly, all the lights in his neighborhood blacked out. All the radios stopped broadcasting. He'd had no idea that his goofing around could cause such a crisis. The world's second most widespread blackout in history plummeted major portions of the northeastern and midwestern United States into darkness. Joey panicked. How could he have done such a terrible thing? Never in a million years would he have hit that light post if he'd known what damage he would do. Would they throw him in jail? Criminy! He was just a kid. He didn't mean for it to happen. His mom would never stop crying. His dad would be so disappointed in him. It was all his fault.

As preposterous as this sounds, and as much as we smile at this true story, stuff like this happens every day in the lives of children. Children are programmed to experiment and to seek cause and effect. Lack of life experience mistakenly leads them to believe that they are personally responsible for coincidental events. Magical Thinking causes people to believe that events have been brought about by their thoughts alone. Even adults reproach themselves with, "If only I had done X, then Y would not have happened," or "I caused him to do Y because I wished it." This is powerful stuff indeed.

Let us now look at my personal story and go to the day of my First Communion.

My parents had fussed over me all day. My parents paid attention to me. Not my older sister or my younger sister. And not even my baby brother. That day had been all about me. I was on center stage. That rarely happened in our family of four kids. I lapped it up. I was a princess for the day. People saw me as the cute one, the good one.

It felt magical, miraculous.

It was a sunny, clear day in May. Family and friends were invited to come to church to see me process down the aisle in a well-practiced line. Dressed in a white frock, white anklets, white patent leather shoes and wearing a crisp veil of netting, I imagined myself radiating my holiness. I was sure I glowed with more holiness than any other girl or boy in those two columns. I was so ready. I had listened, understood, studied, memorized, recited, believed, and now enjoyed—deserved—the culmination of it all. My parents were so proud of me. I was so proud of me.

I was seven years old. I had reached the "Age of Reason," the age at which a child knows the difference between what is right and what is wrong. In order to receive my First Holy Communion, I first needed the sacrament of Penance. I knew the difference between right and wrong. I had to confess my wrong doings, to beg God's forgiveness for being a sinner. I had to ready my soul to receive the body and blood of Jesus.

I had spent hours, weeks, trying to understand my sins. There were little bad actions, called venial sins, which most kids did pretty often. Pulling my sister's hair and sassing my mom were pretty typical venial sins. And there were big, bad acts, like breaking the commandments "Thou shalt not kill" or "Thou shalt not commit adultery."

I figured out most kids never committed these sins. I sure hadn't.

But wait! There was a pretty significant clause about sins. A sin was an action *or a thought* that was not good and holy. So just thinking about doing something bad was a sin, especially if I put a little extra energy into that bad thought. Hmmm, I might be in trouble here.

That year of preparation got me to thinking about all the sins I was committing. This was not a bad thing. I learned that children need to know when they are being kind and when they are not, and to learn to behave better, how to treat others as they would treat themselves. But I was a good girl, so I put a lot of thought into figuring out how I was sinning. Just what would put me into hell for all eternity, or just what would make me feel kind of bad. Guilt was a finely tuned response.

I figured out enough of it. I confessed. I prayed. I was forgiven. I believed. I passed the test and the critical eyes of the good nuns. I received my First Holy Communion that beautiful spring morning.

After the ceremony, we returned to my home, to a party that honored me. My parents had stayed up late the night before, making potato salad and arranging rolled slices of ham on a platter for my aunts, uncles, cousins, and grandparents to feast on. They were celebrating what a good job I had done, what a good girl I was.

It got dark. After everyone left, my very tired but happy mom and dad shooed us to bed. I was exhausted. What a day it had been! My sisters and I knelt on the floor next to our bed and prayed, "Now I lay me down to sleep, I pray thee, Lord, my soul to keep. If I should die before I wake, I pray thee, Lord, my soul to take." I am sure my good-night hug and kiss were especially sweet. I fell asleep with a beatific smile on my face.

I startled awake. I heard my dad's very loud voice. He was crying. I walked into the dining room. My daddy was crying, sobbing and banging his head on the wall. I think I stood there for quite a while before I was noticed. It was probably my grandmother who told me to go back to my bedroom, to get out of the way. I don't recall where my mom was, but I do remember hearing her chant, "Oh, God, no. Oh, God, no."

That night, of all nights, my twenty-three-month-old brother, Bobby, died. I really hadn't given him much thought that entire day. He was a nice baby brother. He made us smile and laugh. He had a bad cold, that was all.

He was the youngest child and the only boy in our family. Why did he die? Why did God take his soul? What made it happen?

Then I figured it out. I had received the body and blood of Jesus that day. So God had taken the body and blood of my brother. It was a reasonable trade. Even though I hadn't intended for that to happen, it obviously happened because of me.

It was my fault. It was so clear. My mother would never stop crying. My dad would be so disappointed because of me. I quickly and unshakably knew that I was personally responsible. It was all because of proud, self-centered me.

I couldn't change it now. But I could change me. I could become the best girl in the world. I could make my parents smile again by being very helpful. I would never be a bother again. Every day I would be obedient, get good grades, do my chores cheerfully.

I was a grown-up seven.

—Paulette Litz

Song of Thanks

When I was febrile and delirious at age five
Mother made me feel worse
with her worried attempts at comfort.

When wounds missed major blood vessels and nerves
on three occasions and even though untended, healed

When free-falling midair through a fat buckeye tree
a convenient limb presented itself for a handhold

When sliding down the face of a cliff
and a vine and a ledge caught me

When the knife thrust and held at my throat
mysteriously was released the night
I wandered, aimless,
into a park at 3:00 a.m.

When inebriated, flipping through vacant space
I slid off a balustrade
and landed on my feet

When Grandfather lovingly held me on his knee
My English-only ears heard
his life story and hard-earned advice in Polish,
and all was clear to me

When intuitively answering questions
kept me in school and illuminated my path

For keeping my marriage together
long enough to raise my children despite reason
while each of us traded grievous hurts

For inspiring me to act
beyond my abilities with kindness, generosity, and mercy
instead of my habitual responses of fear, greed, and cynicism

For the synchronicity of sending people
and staging events at critical junctures
that nurtured, guided, and protected me

For telling me my mission in a dream,
allowing the freedom to accept or reject it
and to choose its context and timing

When walking with our dog on a clear, frigid night,
depressed and alienated,
my name boomed loudly from the ethers,
and my knees buckled

When the birds sing, the wind blows, the rain falls, the trees
sway,
and the crickets and toads chant duets to the hum of the earth

When I stray, when I stumble,
When I laugh, and when I sing
When a poem brings a tear
and a tear begets a poem

When an iridescent green glow emanates from the ground
on a moonless night
and guides my feet home

Then I was with You,
You were with me.
Now the curtain lifts
I see what was always there
I am You; You are Me,
as well as They and We.

—Doug Brozell

REFERENCES

Bartlett, Richard. *Matrix Energetics: The Science and Art of Transformation*. New York: Atria, 2007.

Bradshaw, John. *Homecoming: Reclaiming and Championing Your Inner Child*. New York, NY: Bantam Books, 1990.

Brennan, Barbara. Barbara Brennan School of Healing. http://barbarabrennan.com

Capacchione, Lucia. *Recovery of Your Inner Child*. New York: Simon & Schuster, 1991.

Howard, Christopher. *Turning Passions into Profits: Three Steps to Wealth and Power*. Hoboken, NJ.: Wiley & Sons, 2005.

Dias, Brian G. & Kerry J. Ressler. Parental olfactory experience influences behavior and neural structure in subsequent generations. *Nature Neuroscience* 17, 89–96, 2014.

Hill, Napoleon. *Think and Grow Rich*. Greenwich, Conn.: Fawcett Crest, 1960.

Jung, Carl. Jacobi, Jolande, ed. *Complex, Archetype, Symbol in the Psychology of C.G. Jung*. London: Routledge, 1999.

Lipton, Bruce, PhD. *The Biology of Belief*. Mountain of Love, 2005.

Missildine, W. Hugh. *Your Inner Child of the Past*. New York: Simon and Schuster, 1963.

Moss, Robert. *Dreaming the Soul Back Home: Shamanic Dreaming for Healing and Becoming Whole*. Novato, CA: New World Library, 2012.

Ruiz, Miguel. *The Four Agreements: A Practical Guide to Personal Freedom*. San Rafael, CA: Amber-Allen, 1997.

Vitale, Joe, and Ihaleakala Hew Len. *Zero Limits: The Secret Hawaiian System for Wealth, Health, Peace, and More.* Hoboken, NJ: Wiley, 2007.

Williams, Robert M. *PSYCH-K: The Missing Peace in Your Life.* Crestone, CO: Myrddin Publications, 2004.

Yogananda, Paramahansa. *Autobiography of a Yogi.* Los Angeles, CA: Self-Realization Fellowship, 1974.

INDEX

A

abandonment
 as inner child access point, 45–46
 in session, 116–18
academics. *See* learning
"acting out" defense mechanism, 125
adulthood. *See also* childhood
 making a connection with wounded inner child, 10, 14
 tantrums in, 35–47
 wounded heart recognition in, 5–6
age (participant), 143
anger
 as inner child access point, 38–39
 in session, 74–75, 98, 128–32
annoyance access point, 38–39
anxiety
 as inner child access point, 40–41
 in session, 80–81
appreciation. *See also* gratitude
 and compassion, 213
 in Child-Heart method, 56
approval need strategy, 111–12
attack. *See* trauma
attention
 emotion calling for, 35–38
 in Child-Heart method, 52–53, 56–57
 to life, 22–23
Autobiography of a Yogi, 30
awareness
 as step in Child-Heart method, 31
 in beliefs, 94
ayahuasca (healing ceremony), 92–93

B

being present. *See* presence
beliefs. *See also* strategies, spirituality
    and life definition, 88–89
    as blinders to reality, 89–90
    awareness and choice in, 94
    Child-Heart method session, 95–01
    coming from others, 92–93
    origin of, 90–92
    should, always, never (words) in, 93–94
betrayal access point, 45
Biology of Belief, 88
bullying, 42–43

C

Cancer as a Turning Point, 24
Child-Heart method
    components of, 7
    development background of, 7–8
    multiple child-selves in, 6
    overcoming strategies, 107
    relationship in, 13–4
    signs of two-year-old in, 9
    transformations from, 68–71
Child-Heart method principles, 136–42
Child-Heart method sessions
    baby in utero, 76–79
    complete process, 73–76
    dissociation, 132–33
    highlighting compassion and empathy, 79–85
    involving beliefs, 95–01
    participants' ages, 143
    revealing a strategy, 115–18
    somaticizing defense mechanism, 128–32
    what happens between, 142
Child-Heart method steps
    acceptance, 52
    and learning heart needs, 48–49
    attention and compassion, 52–53, 56–57, 59–60
    building rapport, 65–67
    commitment to, 23, 53, 60–61
    completion, 141–42

courage to step forward, 52
listening with curiosity, 52, 58–59
meditation in, 30–31
noticing two-year-old behaviors, 31
place of imagination, 52, 53–54
presence, 52, 55
spirituality, 52. 55
childhood. *See also* inner child, adulthood
beliefs in, 91–92
best participant age, 143
transition from, 10, 23–25
wounded hearts in, 5–6, 19–20, 153–56
commitment
in Child-Heart method, 7, 60–61
to a relationship with inner child, 14
to self-inquiry, 23
compassion
and appreciation, 139
in Child-Heart method, 7, 52, 56–57
in session, 79–85
confusion
as inner child access point, 46
in session, 128–32
control need strategy, 110–11
courage
in session, 78, 81–82
to begin therapy, 14–15
to face inner child, 31–32
cries of heart. *See* wounded hearts
culture
and beliefs, 88–90, 92–93
and the Child-Heart method, 144
and unattended inner conflicts, 27–28
in session, 83–84
curiosity
in Child-Heart method, 12, 58
to unattended inner conflicts, 27

D

defense mechanisms
"shutting down", 124–25
attacking, striking back, acting out, 125

definitions of, 121

denial, 122–23

dissociation, 125–26

intellectualization, 124

projection, 126–28

session, 128–33

somaticizing, 126

suppression and repression, 123–24

denial (defense mechanism), 122–23

depression access point, 46–47

disappointment access point, 38–39

dissociation

defense mechanism, 125–26

in session, 98–01, 132–33

distraction by life, 22–23

dream of the planet, 26–27

E

embarrassment access point, 42–43

emotion

and wounded heart recognition, 17–20

as access point to inner child, 9, 38–47, 61–65

as call for attention, 35–38

empathy, 79–85

envy access point, 42–43

expectations and needs, 17

F

family

and beliefs, 92

and wounded heart recognition, 18

in session, 128–132

fear

and wounded heart recognition, 9

as inner child access point, 40–41

cultural conditioning and, 27–28

in session, 77, 80–85

Four Agreements, 88

frustration

as inner child access point, 38–39

in session, 73–76

G

God. *See* spirituality
gratitude. *See also* appreciation
    in Child-Heart method, 57–58, 67
    song of thanks, 157–59
grief access point, 41–42
guilt access point, 43–44

H

happiness, 61–63, 75–76, 141
helplessness access point, 44
Hew Len, Ihaleakela, 58
"hiding who you are" belief, 95–97
Hill, Napoleon, 137
hopelessness
    as inner child access point, 44
    in *ayahuasca*, 93
humiliation access point, 42–43

I

imaginal world. *See also* meditation
    in Child-Heart method, 7, 52, 53–54
    in session, 7, 52, 115–17
    power of, 136–38
    uniqueness of, 14
imagination
    and childhood, 52, 154
    in Child heart method, 61
    in session, 79–82, 115–17
    use of, 137
inner child. *See also* two-year-old, childhood
    and beliefs, 88–90
    asking questions of, 138–39
    defense mechanisms, 121–28
    emotions as access points for, 38–47, 62–65
    holding back and playing, 139–41
    manifestations of, 9–10
    scholarly work on, 12–14
inner child access points
    abandonment, confusion, 45–46
    anger,annoyance, disappointment, frustration, irritation, 38–39

anxiety fear, worry, 40–41
betrayal, 45
depression, 46–47
embarrassment, humiliation, shame, 42–43
emotion, 9
envy, jealousy, 42
grief, sadness, 41–42
guilt, regret, remorse, 43–44
helplessness, hopelessness, powerlessness, 44
loneliness, 44–45
negative emotions, 63–65
positive emotions, 62–63
resentment, 39–40
intellectualization defense mechanism, 124
invitation of child-self, 7
irritation access point, 38–39

J

jealousy access point, 42–43
journaling
and learning heart needs, 49
and self-reflection, 14–15, 33
beliefs, 102–03
Child-Heart method steps, 71
commitment to, 23
defense mechanisms, 133–34
emotions from sessions, 86
strategy, 120
what grabs attention, 36

L

learning
and academics, 29–31
and listening, 29–31
and spirituality, 29–31
and the dream of the planet, 26–27
from tantrums, 47–48
heart's needs, 47–49
LeShan, Lawrence, 24–25
life transitions and wounded hearts, 23–25
listening

and learning, 29–31
to wounded hearts, 20–22
with curiosity, 52, 58
loneliness access point, 44–45
lost children, 13, 17

M

meditation. *See also* imaginal world
and being a practitioner, 143
in Child-Heart method, 30–31, 52, 53–54
mind
and unattended inner conflicts, 26–27
as authority, 29–31

N

needs and expectations, 17
negative emotions
and beliefs and strategies, 107–08
as inner child access point, 38–47, 63–65
numbness (inner child), 9

O

optimism, 90
overreactions (emotional), 37–38

P

pain
in facing inner child, 31–32
in inner child's heart, 14
in session, 78–79, 128–32
patience (in Child-Heart method), 58–59, 66
pessimism, 90
pets and loneliness, 44–45
physical symptoms
and unattended inner conflicts, 24
in session, 115–16
of wounded hearts, 19
somaticizing defense mechanism, 126–27
play, 139–41
post-traumatic stress disorder (PTSD), 125–26
power of belief, 88

powerlessness access point, 44
presence
    in Child-Heart method, 7, 9, 52, 55
    in session, 81, 95
principles (Child-Heart method), 136–42
projection defense mechanism, 126–28
protection methods
    and strategies, 114
    courage to confront, 14–15

Q

questions (to inner child), 138–39

R

rapport (in Child-Heart method), 65–67
regret access point, 43–44
relationship
    and unattended inner conflicts, 25
    committed, 14
    in Child-Heart method, 13
remorse access point, 43–44
repression defense mechanism, 123–24
resentment access point, 39–40
right and wrong strategy, 108–09

S

sadness
    as inner child access point, 41–42
    in session, 73–74, 82
safety
    creating a place of, 51–52, 54–55
    in Child heart method, 53
    in session, 75, 81–85, 129–31
    sense of, 40, 53, 139–40
self-reflection
    and journaling, 15–16
    and learning heart needs, 48–49
    commitment to, 23
    importance for recognizing wounded heart, 10–13
shame
    as inner child access point, 42–43

in session, 98–00

"shutting down" defense mechanism, 124–25

Socratic method, 48

somaticizing defense mechanism, 126, 128–32

spirituality. *See also* beliefs

    and the mind, 29–31

    and wounded hearts, 19–20

    in Child-Heart method, 52, 55

storytelling strategy, 112–13

strategies (from heart wounds). *See also* beliefs

    and negative emotions, 107–08

    session, 115–18

    sources of, 108–14

    types of, 105–07

striking back defense mechanism, 125

suppression defense mechanism, 123–24

survival strategy, 113–14

T

tantrums

    as sign of wounded heart, 5

    learning hearts needs from, 47–48

    recognition of, 35–47

Tao Te Ching, 119

Think and Grow Rich, 137

transformations

    and sessions, 135–36

    from the Child-Heart method, 68–71

trauma

    and defense mechanisms, 121–22

    and repression, 123–24

trauma strategy, 109–10

two-year-old. *See also* inner child

    and adult tantrums, 35–47

    as first step in Child-Heart method, 9–10

    noticing behaviors of, 31

U

unconsciousness and wounded hearts, 25

undefended heart, 32–33, 135, 145, 151–52

utero (baby in), 74–79

V

vulnerability in wounded hearts, 23–25
visualization, 54, 119, 137
Vitale, Joe, 58

W

words and beliefs, 93–94
worry
    as inner child access point, 40–41
    in session, 77
wounded heart recognition
    and cultural norms, 27–28
    and vulnerability, 23–25
    from strategies, 108–114
    going unheard, 25
    helpful for both therapists and clients, 13
    importance of self-reflection to, 10–13
    tantrums, 35–47
wounded hearts
    examples of, 5–6
    listening to, 20–22
    manifestations of, 17–20
    universality of, 145

Y

"you're okay" belief, 98–101

Z

Zero Limits, 58

ABOUT THE AUTHOR

Anne Uemura, PhD, has many traditional achievements in her background. After receiving her bachelor's and master's degrees in Philosophy, she taught at the college level for ten years. Her Socratic style led her to question the direction of her own life, which led to a PhD in Clinical Psychology at University of Maine. A predoctoral fellowship at UC-San Francisco followed by a postdoctoral fellowship at UC-Berkeley situated her permanently in California. After thirteen years as a counseling psychologist for troubled, promising students in workshops, group, and individual counseling at UC-Berkeley, Anne retired to a small private practice in Napa, California. The leisure of this period of midlife afforded her the opportunity to explore nontraditional studies and training.

Anne sees her life as a testimony to the riches of achievement through traditional means. But more important, she is eager to tell you about how much more there is when you move to the out-of-the-box principles and concepts that eventually led her to write her groundbreaking book, *Listen to the Cries of Your Heart*. Exploration into and teaching about the treasures of midlife comes directly from Anne's personal and professional experiences. The personal ones include an empty nest, marriage, divorce, retirement, illness, and death among friends and family. The professional ones include studies with Toltec teachers (former apprentices of Don Miguel, author of *The Four Agreements*), Ericksonian hypnotists, Barbara Brennan's energy science, Joe Vitale and Bob Proctor, participants in *The Secret*, and enlightened teachers in books and in person. She embraces the positive model of life coaching as well as current change technologies of Psych-K (based on the *Biology of Beliefs*), Chris Howard's Neurological Repatterning, and Richard Bartlett's Matrix Energetics.

Anne's teaching reflects a profound appreciation of the uniqueness of her life path and the need to honor the same in others. In the end, each person's search for more in life is about finding the more inside, whether you call it heart or potential. In order to move forward, however, Anne emphasizes the influence of early childhood experiences and societal conditioning on beliefs, values, and models. She combines the appreciation of the traditional psychotherapy model of combing through past traumas with the necessity of moving forward. This means releasing the limitations of the past and learning to be "at cause" everywhere in life. All the practices and techniques gathered from cutting-edge technologies and from ancient teachings enhance her offerings.

Knowing full well that she's a work in progress, Anne is pleased to recognize this state as her chosen destiny. Her youthful spirit is ever open, always curious, and growing in awareness and in loving-kindness. She delights in seeing people blooming fresh versions of themselves and inspiring others by their example.

Anne offers individual coaching, workshops, classes, presentations, and monthly newsletters.

Learn more at http://Childheartmethod.com.

CPSIA information can be obtained
at www.ICGtesting.com
Printed in the USA
FFOW02n1614260716
26243FF

9 780997 654523